THE PROPHETS
AND KINGS

The Bible for
School and Home

by J. Paterson Smyth

The Book of Genesis

Moses and the Exodus

Joshua and the Judges

The Prophets and Kings

*When the Christ Came:
The Highlands of Galilee*

*When the Christ Came:
The Road to Jerusalem*

St. Matthew

St. Mark

The Bible for School and Home

THE PROPHETS
AND KINGS

by

J. Paterson Smyth

YESTERDAY'S CLASSICS

ITHACA, NEW YORK

This edition, first published in 2017 by Yesterday's Classics, an imprint of Yesterday's Classics, LLC, is an unabridged republication of the text originally published by Sampson Low, Marston & Co., Ltd. For the complete listing of the books that are published by Yesterday's Classics, please visit www.yesterdaysclassics.com. Yesterday's Classics is the publishing arm of the Baldwin Online Children's Literature Project which presents the complete text of hundreds of classic books for children at www.mainlesson.com.

ISBN: 978-1-63334-011-4

Yesterday's Classics, LLC
PO Box 339
Ithaca, NY 14851

CONTENTS

GENERAL INTRODUCTION

I

This series of books is intended for two classes of teachers:

1. *For Teachers in Week Day and Sunday Schools.* For these each book is divided into complete lessons. The lesson will demand preparation. Where feasible there should be diligent use of commentaries and of any books indicated in the notes. *As a general rule* I think the teacher should not bring the book at all to his class if he is capable of doing without it. He should make copious notes of the subject. The lesson should be thoroughly studied and digested beforehand, with all the additional aids at his disposal, and it should come forth at the class warm and fresh from his own heart and brain. But I would lay down no rigid rule about the use of the Lesson Book. To some it may be a burden to keep the details of a long lesson in the memory; and, provided the subject has been very carefully studied, the Lesson Book, with its salient points carefully marked in coloured pencil, may be a considerable help. Let each do what seems best in his particular case, only taking care to satisfy his conscience that it is not done through

1

laziness, and that he can really do best for his class by the plan which he adopts.

2. *For Parents* who would use it in teaching their children at home. They need only small portions, brief little lessons of about ten minutes each night. For these each chapter is divided into short sections. I should advise that on the first night only the Scripture indicated should be read, with some passing remarks and questions to give a grip of the story. That is enough. Then night after night go on with the teaching, taking as much or as little as one sees fit.

I have not written out the teaching in full as a series of readings which could be read over to the child without effort or thought. With this book in hand a very little preparation and adaptation will enable one to make the lesson more interesting and more personal and to hold the child's attention by questioning. Try to get his interest. Try to make him talk. Make the lesson conversational. Don't preach.

II

HINTS FOR TEACHING

An ancient Roman orator once laid down for his pupils the three-fold aim of a teacher:

1. *Placere* (to interest).

2. *Docere* (to teach).

3. *Movere* (to move).

1. To interest the audience (in order to teach them).

2. To teach them (in order to move them).

3. To move them to action.

On these three words of his I hang a few suggestions on the teaching of this set of Lessons.

1. *Placere (to interest)*

I want especially to insist on attention to this rule. Some teachers seem to think that to interest the pupils is a minor matter. It is not a minor matter and the pupils will very soon let you know it. Believe me, it is no waste of time to spend hours during the week in planning to excite their interest to the utmost. Most of the complaints of inattention would cease at once if the teacher would give more study to rousing their interest. After all, there is little use in knowing the facts of your subject, and being anxious about the souls of the pupils, if all the time that you are teaching, these pupils are yawning and taking no interest in what you say. I know some have more aptitude for teaching than others. Yet, after considerable experience of teachers whose lesson was a weariness to the flesh, and of teachers who never lost attention for a moment, I am convinced, on the whole, that the power to interest largely depends on the previous preparation.

Therefore do not content yourself with merely studying the teaching of this series. Read widely and freely. Read not only commentaries, but books that will give local interest and colour—books that will throw valuable sidelights on your sketch.

But more than reading is necessary. You know the meaning of the expression, *"Put yourself in his place."* Practise that in every Bible story, using your imagination, living in the scene, experiencing, as far as you can, every feeling of the actors. To some this is no effort at all. They feel their cheeks flushing and their eyes growing moist as they project themselves involuntarily into the scene before them. But though it be easier to some than to others, it is in some degree possible to all, and the interest of the lesson largely depends on it. I have done my best in these books to help the teacher in this respect. But no man can help another much. Success will depend entirely on the effort to "put yourself in his place."

In reading the Bible chapter corresponding to each lesson, I suggest that the teacher should read part of the chapter, rather than let the pupils tire themselves by "reading round." My experience is that this "reading round" is a fruitful source of listlessness. When his verse is read, the pupil can let his mind wander till his turn comes again, and so he loses all interest. I have tried, with success, varying the monotony. I would let them read the first round of verses in order; then I would make them read out of the regular order, as I called their names; and sometimes, if the lesson were long, I would again and again interrupt by reading a group of verses myself, making remarks as I went on. To lose their interest is fatal.

I have indicated also in the lessons that you should not unnecessarily give information yourself. Try to question it *into* them. If you tell them facts which they have just read, they grow weary. If you ask a question, and then answer it yourself when they miss it, you cannot keep their attention. Send your questions around in every sort of order, or want of order. Try to puzzle them—try to surprise them. Vary the form of the question, if not answered, and always feel it to be a defeat if you ultimately fail in getting the answer you want.

2. Docere (to teach)

You interest the pupil in order that you may *teach*. Therefore teach definitely the Lesson that is set you. Do not be content with interesting him. Do not be content either with drawing spiritual teaching. Teach the facts before you. Be sure that God has inspired the narration of them for some good purpose.

When you are dealing with Old Testament characters, do not try to shirk or to condone evil in them. They were not faultless saints. They were men like ourselves, whom God was helping and bearing with, as He helps and bears with us, and the interest of the story largely depends on the pupil realizing this.

In the Old Testament books of this series you will find very full chapters written on the Creation, the Fall, the Flood, the election of Jacob, the Sun standing still, the slaughter of Canaanites, and other such subjects. In connection with these I want to say something that

5

especially concerns teachers. Your pupils, now or later, can hardly avoid coming in contact with the flippant scepticism so common nowadays, which makes jests at the story of the sun standing still, and talks of the folly of believing that all humanity was condemned because Eve ate an apple thousands of years ago. This flippant tone is "in the air." They will meet with it in their companions, in the novels of the day, in popular magazine articles on their tables at home. You have, many of you, met with it yourselves; you know how disturbing it is; and you probably know, too, that much of its influence on people arises from the narrow and unwise teaching of the Bible in their youth. Now you have no right to ignore this in your teaching of the Bible. You need not talk of Bible difficulties and their answers. You need not refer to them at all. But teach the truth that will take the sting out of these difficulties when presented in after-life.

To do this requires trouble and thought. We have learned much in the last fifty years that has thrown new light for us on the meaning of some parts of the Bible; which has, at any rate, made doubtful some of our old interpretations of it. We must not ignore this. There are certain traditional theories which some of us still insist on teaching as God's infallible truth, whereas they are really only human opinions about it, which may possibly be mistaken. As long as they are taught as human opinions, even if we are wrong, the mistake will do no harm. But if things are taught as God's infallible truth, to be believed on peril of doubting God's Word, it may do grave mischief, if in after-life the pupil find them seriously disputed, or perhaps false. A shallow, unthinking man, finding part of his teaching false, which has been associated in his mind with the most solemn sanctions of religion, is in danger of letting the whole go. Thus many of our young people drift into hazy doubt about the Bible. Then we get troubled about their beliefs, and give them books of Christian evidences to win them back by explaining that what was taught them in childhood was not *quite* correct, and needs now to be modified by a broader and slightly different view. But we go on as before with the younger generation, and expose them in their turn to the same difficulties.

Does it not strike you that, instead of this continual planning to win men back from unbelief, it might be worth while to try the other method of not exposing them to unbelief? Give them the more careful and intelligent teaching at first, and so prepare them to meet the difficulties by-and-by.

I have no wish to advocate any so-called "advanced" teaching. Much of such teaching I gravely object to. But there are truths of which there is no question amongst thoughtful people, which somehow are very seldom taught to the young, though ignorance about them in after-life leads to grave doubt and misunderstanding. Take, for example, the gradual, progressive nature of God's teaching in Scripture, which makes the Old Testament teaching as a whole lower than that of the New. This is certainly no doubtful question, and the knowledge of it is necessary for an intelligent study of

Scripture. I have dealt with it where necessary in some of the books of this series.

I think, too, our teaching on what may seem to us doubtful questions should be more fearless and candid. If there are two different views each held by able and devout men, do not teach your own as the infallibly true one, and ignore or condemn the other. For example, do not insist that the order of creation must be accurately given in the first chapter of Genesis. You may think so; but many great scholars, with as deep a reverence for the Bible as you have, think that inspired writers were circumscribed by the science of their time. Do not be too positive that the story of the Fall *must be* an exactly literal narrative of facts. If you believe that it is I suppose you must tell your pupil so. But do not be afraid to tell him also that there are good and holy and scholarly men who think of it as a great old-world allegory, like the parable of the Prodigal Son, to teach in easy popular form profound lessons about sin. Endeavor in your Bible teaching "to be thoroughly truthful: to assert nothing as certain which is not certain, nothing as probable which is not probable, and nothing as more probable than it is." Let the pupil see that there are some things that we cannot be quite sure about, and let him gather insensibly from your teaching the conviction that truth, above all things, is to be loved and sought, and that religion has never anything to fear from discovering the truth. If we could but get this healthy, manly, common-sense attitude adopted now in teaching the Bible to young people, we should, with

God's blessing, have in the new generation a stronger and more intelligent faith.

3. Movere (to move)

All your teaching is useless unless it have this object: to move the heart, to rouse the affections toward the love of God, and the will toward the effort after the blessed life. You interest in order to teach. You teach in order to move. *That* is the supreme object. Here the teacher must be left largely to his own resources. One suggestion I offer: don't preach. At any rate, don't preach much lest you lose grip of your pupils. You have their attention all right while their minds are occupied by a carefully prepared lesson; but wait till you close your Bible, and, assuming a long face, begin, "And now, boys," etc. and straightway they know what is coming, and you have lost them in a moment.

Do not change your tone at the application of your lesson. Try to keep the teaching still conversational. Try still in this more spiritual part of your teaching to question into them what you want them to learn. Appeal to the judgment and to the conscience. I can scarce give a better example than that of our Lord in teaching the parable of the Good Samaritan. He first interested His pupil by putting His lesson in an attractive form, and then He did not append to it a long, tedious moral. He simply asked the man before Him, "Which of these three *thinkest thou?*"—i.e., "What do you think about it?" The interest was still kept up. The man, pleased at the appeal to his judgment, replied promptly, "He that showed mercy on him;" and on the instant came the quick rejoinder, "Go, and do thou likewise." Thus the lesson ends. Try to work on that model.

Now, while forbidding preaching to your pupils, may I be permitted a little preaching myself? This series of lessons is intended for Sunday schools as well as week-day schools. It is of Sunday-school teachers I am thinking in what I am now about to say. I cannot escape the solemn feeling of the responsibility of every teacher for the children in his care. Some of these children have little or no religious influence exerted on them for the whole week except in this one hour with you. Do not make light of this work. Do not get to think, with good-natured optimism, that all the nice, pleasant children in your class are pretty sure to be Christ's soldiers and servants by-and-by. Alas! for the crowds of these nice, pleasant children, who, in later life, wander away from Christ into the ranks of evil. Do not take this danger lightly. Be anxious; be prayerful; be terribly in earnest, that the one hour in the week given you to use be wisely and faithfully used.

But, on the other hand, be very hopeful too, because of the love of God. He will not judge you hardly. Remember that He will bless very feeble work, if it be your best. Remember that He cares infinitely more for the children's welfare than you do, and, therefore, by His grace, much of the teaching about which you are despondent may bring forth good fruit in the days to come. Do you know the lines about "The Noisy Seven"?—

"I wonder if he remembers—
    Our sainted teacher in heaven—
The class in the old grey schoolhouse,
    Known as the 'Noisy Seven'?

"I wonder if he remembers
    How restless we used to be.
Or thinks we forget the lesson
    Of Christ and Gethsemane?

"I wish I could tell the story
    As he used to tell it then;
I'm sure that, with Heaven's blessing,
    It would reach the hearts of men.

"I often wish I could tell him,
    Though we caused him so much pain
By our thoughtless, boyish frolic,
    His lessons were not in vain.

"I'd like to tell him how Willie,
    The merriest of us all,
From the field of Balaclava
    Went home at the Master's call.

"I'd like to tell him how Ronald,
    So brimming with mirth and fun,
Now tells the heathen of India
    The tale of the Crucified One.

"I'd like to tell him how Robert,
    And Jamie, and George, and 'Ray,'
Are honoured in the Church of God—
    The foremost men of their day.

"I'd like, yes, I'd like to tell him
  What his lesson did for me;
And how I am trying to follow
  The Christ of Gethsemane.

"Perhaps he knows it already,
  For Willie has told him, maybe,
That we are all coming, coming
  Through Christ of Gethsemane.

"How many besides I know not
  Will gather at last in heaven,
The fruit of that faithful sowing,
  But the sheaves are already seven."

PREFATORY NOTE

Uphilas, their bishop, when translating the Old Testament for the Goths long ago, omitted altogether the four books of Samuel and Kings lest the stories of battle should stimulate too much the fierce spirit of the barbarians. In facing the task before me now I could almost wish that it were possible to imitate Bishop Uphilas, though for a very different reason.

For what is one to do with this vast mass of sacred literature, nearly thirty books, more than three-fourths of the whole Old Testament, that is covered by the story of the Prophets and Kings? How can one deal with it in a single Book of Lessons? One might perhaps tell of the kings alone, but it would be of little value leaving out their prophets.

Besides, I want to make the prophets stand out in their places, each in his own environment, each under his own kings—to make the pupil acquainted with them and interested in them as men, in the hope that he may thus be more induced to acquaint himself and interest himself in some of their writings and also be more likely to understand what they had in their minds. The prophets, except Isaiah, are very little read. Groups of sermons and speeches taken out of their setting in time and place with little or no indication as to author or environment are not likely to be interesting.

Now this is a very large undertaking. Covering so wide a field, lessons in detail are clearly impossible. After full consideration I have decided to treat the whole subject in bold, broad outline, omitting all but the salient features and trying to keep the personal interest by making it into a series of biographies.

The teacher will need very careful preparation. One difficulty he will find is that instead of giving, as in previous volumes, one chapter or section of Scripture to be dealt with I have sometimes had to dip into several chapters for one lesson. These he must study carefully beforehand. I should suggest that either before or after telling the story he should select from the Scripture portions indicated as much as the class will bear without weariness. I do not think it at all desirable to tell the stories merely as I have given them, without fastening them on to the words of Scripture. He must use his own discretion as to whether it is better to do this Scripture reading before or after the story.

One other suggestion. If he has really interested his class and made them talk, he will often find it difficult to get his lesson finished in the time. Therefore, if not bound by programme, I should advise him not to hurry. One of these lessons might often expand into two. The whole subject covers such a large expanse of Scripture that it is well worth taking plenty of time.

LESSON I

SAUL'S CORONATION

The Necessary Parts of

1 Samuel IX., XI., XIV., XV.

We have now come to the fourth volume of the Old Testament story. We have gone through the events of Genesis, then the remaining Pentateuch history as it centred around the life of Moses; then came the wild rough days of the reign of the Judges and now we are to follow the fortunes of Israel in the days of the Prophets and Kings. I wonder if you have by this time found out the use of learning all this ancient history. Is it of any more use than the learning of American or English history? Do you think God was more behind the Jewish history than behind these? I do not. I think God is equally behind all history. As much behind the Norman Conquest and the Spanish Armada and the American Revolution as behind any historical event in Old Testament story. The only difference that I can see is that God showed Himself in the one history, that He might teach men to look for Him in the other histories.

The Israelite history had inspired historians, not always very wise or very clever, but with a deep insight into the ways of God, whereas the modern history is often told only by mere essayists and newspaper writers, and secular historians, who only tell of the incidental and outward appearances and occurrences, and have not learned the deep insight which sees God behind all. If our study of God working behind the scenes of Jewish history teaches us to look for Him also behind the scenes of all other history, I think it will have been worth doing.

§ 1. The Lost Asses

We begin at the ninth chapter of 1 Samuel, when our last book—the "Story of the Judges"—closes. That story told us, how in the days of Samuel, the "last of the Judges," Israel had demanded of God a king. And you remember how in the last scene of that story, the curtain fell on the old prophet quietly returning to Ramah, waiting on the hill of God till the king should come.

*   *   *   *   *   *   *   *

About ten years have passed, ten waiting years, when the curtain rises again on a very ordinary scene. A drove of asses gone astray on the mountains and a young farmer's son with his dark Edomite servant[1] setting off to find them. A goodly youth was this young farmer's son, "among the children of Israel there was not

---

[1] The Jewish Talmud says that he was the afterwards famous or infamous Doeg the Edomite.

a goodlier person." But except for his fine appearance there seemed nothing especially to notice in him or his story here. It seems quite an ordinary story. He consulted with his servant whether they should climb the hill to Ramah. He talked to the girls going to the village well. He heard of a prophet holding a religious ceremony in the village, and he thought perhaps this prophet might be able by some magical power to tell him about the asses. Does it not seem just like an ordinary newspaper account of ordinary chance things happening? It chanced that the asses went astray one day and that Saul and not another went off to seek them. It chanced that on that day the people of Ramah many miles away invited Samuel to offer sacrifice. It chanced that Saul took that very direction, that he met the girls at the well, that he took their advice and went up to Ramah, little dreaming who was before him—little dreaming that God was sending him, and that the unknown "seer" on the hill was Israel's great prophet, looking out with his dim, old eyes for the king who should be.

God was behind all those chances. One wonders if He is behind all chances, such curious things happen to us sometimes "by chance." By chance we went by this or that tram or train. By chance we met this or that person—and sometimes we find that our whole after life was affected by that chance. A girl meets a friend who changes her whole life course, a man meets a girl who afterwards becomes his wife. Does anything happen by chance? I don't know. All this life of ours is solemn and mysterious and wonderful, and God is behind and over it all.

Now picture to yourself that scene at the gate of the little town—Saul coming carelessly up the hill seeking his asses, and the old prophet watching him with an admiration and wonder and growing excitement as the feeling deepened in his heart that this splendid young countryman is the coming king. I think he fell in love with him right straight away. I think in spite of all Saul's faults the old man loved him tenderly all his days, more than he ever loved David. We read afterwards how he watched over him, and prayed for him, and mourned for him when he went wrong. It is very touching this tenderness of Samuel for the man who was coming to remove him from being chief in Israel. And the thought of all that makes us watch with deeper interest the first meeting of the two.

What a wonderful day that was for Saul when he learned for the first time that God had a life plan for him, a great, glorious, beautiful life plan—when Samuel talked alone with him of the great future, and anointed him king in the name of the Lord—when the wondering youth returned to his farm keeping the great secret hidden in his heart. And more wonderful still when he met the band of young prophets singing to Jehovah, and immediately the Spirit of the Lord came upon Saul, and God gave him another heart. God gave him another heart! What do you understand by that? Surely that was to make him nobler and fuller for his great life work. Already his heart was full of wonder and excitement, but now all in a moment there came on him a new feeling, a consciousness of thoughts and desires altogether different, higher, grander, nobler. Does God do all this in our day? Yes, just the same—to the young girl kneeling at her first Communion, to the young college student on his ordination day—to the man suddenly converted from a life of sin—to the young husband and wife on the day of their marriage—new hopes and thoughts and desires for good come to prepare them for their future life work. Often they disappoint God in spite of it as Saul did. But that does not make God's help less real.

§ 2. God Save the King!

Chapter x. 17, etc. Now a few months afterwards we have a brilliant picture on the plains at Mizpeh. Samuel's message has gone out through the land, and all the warriors of Israel have come together, and the plain is dotted over with tents, and bright with the standards of the tribes, and all the people are keenly excited, for they all come for the election of their king. They do not know who it is to be. They gather around the prophet and hear God's word, and with solemn sense of God's presence they begin the ceremony of drawing lots.

First all the tribes assemble, and the lot falls on the tribe of Benjamin, and the people solemnly feel that God is guiding them. Then the other tribes stand back and watch the families of Benjamin assemble. The family of Matri is chosen. Then the excitement grows deeper as the lot drawing goes on till at last the rumour spreads rapidly through the camp that Saul the son of Kish is marked out by the lot as God's chosen King of Israel. "Who is this Saul?" "What is he like?" Of course every one was full of curiosity. But he had hidden himself, too modest perhaps, or perhaps too much afraid of this great responsibility. At last they found him. It was a thrilling moment when Samuel led him forth. I want you to use your imagination and let your eyes rest on him, as he first appears before the people on his Coronation Day at Mizpeh—this handsome, athletic young giant in the full pride of his youth and strength. In stately presence he stood before them every inch a king. "Amongst the children of Israel, there was not a goodlier person, from his shoulders upward he was taller than any of the people." No wonder the desire of Israel should be upon him in these rude, heroic days, when strength of limb and splendid appearances were the great passport to success. No wonder the crowd burst into enthusiasm when they saw him, and shouted together in loud, glad acclaim, "God save the King!" How the heart of Saul would stir within him at the cry. Ah! it was a grand start in life that God had given that young king. Alas that he did not use it well!

§ 3. The Fiery Cross

Chapter xi. Again the scene changes. We are in Gibeah of Saul, the young king's native village, and we find the king back at the plough-tail again! These are wild, desolate times for Israel. No time for palaces and crowns and royal splendour with the fierce tribes of Ammon and Amalek and Philistia closing in around them, and holding the chief fortresses in the land. Like Shamgar and Gideon in the judges' days, like

Cincinnatus at Rome working on his farm, like King Alfred in England in the shepherd's hut, the king of Israel is at the plough-tail biding his time.

And now his time is come. It is evening, and he is driving back his team of oxen when suddenly he is startled by the deep wailing of a crowd, "What means it?" he asked. And the people tell him, "The Ammonites have surrounded our friends in Jabesh, there is no escape. They are about to put out the right eyes of the men." Then "the Spirit of God came upon Saul, and his anger was kindled greatly." Don't you like that expression? All fierce, righteous indignation for the sake of others is the work of God's spirit. The schoolboy who for the sake of some smaller boy thrashes the bully of the school is doing God's work. It is only selfish anger and fighting for slights done to yourself that are sin. In a moment Saul has struck down the bullocks of his team, and is cutting their bleeding-flesh in little pieces before the people. "Take these pieces North and South and East and West to every village and every town. Tell them, if you are not at the trysting-place with the king when he starts for Jabesh thus shall it be done to your cattle too." Is not it a stirring picture—the fierce anger of the young king and the new hope of the downtrodden people— the messengers with the bleeding flesh, speeding over the hills of Benjamin like the runners of Roderick Dhu with the fiery cross in the *Lady of the Lake*, a picture of righteous wrath and unselfish help, that was good for them all.

Of course they swept the Ammonites before them. There is no such stimulus to victory as rage about another's wrong. And it is a beautiful conclusion to the victory, that, when the army wanted to kill the men who had despised him at his coronation, Saul nobly replied, "Not a single man of them shall die, for God has been to-day fighting for Israel!"

§ 4. *The Centre of Life*

The scene changes again—and again—and again. But we cannot follow all the changing fortunes of Israel. You see Israel was like England in the times of the Danes, or like Spain in the Moorish days with the enemy holding the fastnesses all through the land. Moab and Ammon oppressed them on the east, Edom and Amalek on the south, and, in the very heart of the land, the big, stupid Philistines whom Samson used to fight and mock, and ridicule. There was no lack of wars, and of romantic adventures like that of Jonathan and his armour-bearer scaling the tower (*ch.* xiv.). But we have to get the whole life of Saul into two chapters, and we are concerned with Saul's character and the lessons of his life more than with the fights and skirmishes of the tribes.

Up to this time it looks as if all were going well with him. God had called him to a high position, given him great opportunities, splendid endowments, attractive gifts of body and mind, and over all the great gift of His Holy Spirit to lift up and ennoble his life. With such a start one would think he could not go wrong. Yet the Bible seems to teach us that something else is needed, something down deep in the inner nature of the man himself. God wants greatly to bless us, but He must leave our wills free. He cannot just pull strings to make us act like marionettes upon the stage. Our great dignity is that we have at the centre of our being our power to decide, so that the man with the grand start in life can lose it, and the poor struggler with very few advantages can rise to a noble life with the help of God which is around him. That is where Saul's life touches our own. That is what makes his story so solemn and sad. For he was just like many of ourselves, not a monster, but an ordinary, middling sort of man. I don't think he really cared very much about God, or longed above everything else to please Him, and to be good. And all the advantages and opportunities, and gifts and endowment that God gave him could not make up for that. What a man feels and desires with regard to God is the one important thing. Up to this Saul had shown up well. But that does not always mean that things are right within. When no sharp test comes—when there is happiness and comfort, and freedom from temptation—many people show up well; but the testing is bound to come some time.

§ 5. *The Rejection of Saul*

The first evil recorded of him (*ch.* xiii.) is not very easy to understand. We do not really know in what his sin consisted. We are told that Saul and his men were out on the battlefield waiting for Samuel to come and offer sacrifices, and bless the army. That because Samuel did not come in time, Saul offered the sacrifice himself. The wrong seems to have been in the spirit of the act, not merely in usurping the priestly office. David offered sacrifices without any blame. Judging from the whole story one feels that Saul must have acted irreverently or disobeyed some definite command (see *v.* 13). Imagine a King in our day in like circumstances, after waiting vainly for a clergyman, rising up at last in irreverent impatience to consecrate the Holy Communion himself, as a matter of form to be gone through, or a superstitious rite that might bring good luck to the army. If Saul did anything like this it would indicate a very wrong attitude towards God. And as you watch Samuel's fierce anger and solemn denunciation of the act, you must see that this act was in some way a clear proof of Saul's wilfulness and disobedience.

Chapter xiv. tells an incident that puts Saul back into the ignorant superstition of Jephthah's time. To ensure victory he makes a vow to kill whoever shall taste of food, and because Jonathan, who did not know this, tasted some honey he wanted to kill him. It looks a little like the beginning of that half insane spirit of his later life.

Chapter xv. tells of his next open disobedience. It is difficult to speak of it briefly, since it tells of a thing that puzzles us, the destruction of a whole tribe, commanded it is said by God. We have already more than once considered this difficulty before. You remember that God's teaching of the world was gradual, as men could bear it. Stern, righteous men inspired to hate and loathe the horrible abominations around them declared the will of God as far as they could see it. It does not follow that they were always right. Perhaps God did desire the destruction of the Amalekites. They were very impure, wicked people. Perhaps you will say that they were very ignorant, too, and that it was hard that they should be cut off in their ignorance and sin. If so, remember that they lived still after death, and were still in the hands of God in that new life, and that the judge of all the earth will do right, there as well as here. Don't forget that the men of the old world were as children in the great gradual school of God, that it was only at the coming of our Lord that the full light came. Therefore if we want to judge of any Old Testament command, we must always bring it to the light of our Lord's fuller teaching in the Gospels.

But at any rate Saul and the people believed that the destruction of wicked Amalek was God's will for them. And they knew that they were forbidden to win booty for themselves. They were God's crusaders, consecrated to an awful mission of judgment to sweep away the abominations polluting the earth. But they must not make profit out of it. That would spoil the grandeur and holiness of their terrible task. They must not touch the spoil. This was the command that Saul deliberately broke. He spared the king and the best of the cattle. Not for mercy, for he had destroyed all the refuse and useless, and had killed the common people, young and old.

He was evidently pleased with himself, and set up for himself a monument at Carmel (xv. 12). But one day on the homeward march his heart grew suddenly troubled, as the grim old prophet Samuel appeared suddenly in the camp. Nervously, with suspicious haste, he hurries to tell him:—

"I have obeyed the commandment of the Lord."

But he trembles at the sternness of the face before him.

"What meaneth then this bleating of sheep, and lowing of oxen in mine ears?"

"Oh! the people have done that, to sacrifice unto the Lord." Then the king stands silent. He knows well what is coming from that stern, upright judge, who never sought even a shoe latchet for himself. Like a lightning flash the quick judgment fell.

"Behold! to obey is better than sacrifice and to hearken than the fat of rams. Because thou hast rejected the word of the Lord, He hath also rejected thee from being king."

Ah! things had got very bad since that day, perhaps twenty years ago, when he had presented that splendid young king to the people at Mizpeh. Probably in many other ways not recorded he had seen the wrong attitude of the heart of Saul. Now he was so utterly grieved and disappointed, that he went away and refused to see Saul any more till the day of his death—till the day when his spirit came back from Hades to confirm the king's doom. Do you think Samuel was too stern? Ah! look at him, that dear old man returning to his lonely house at Ramah, more miserable about it all than Saul himself. He could not forget him, nor the early days, nor the noble qualities that he once possessed.

Continually the cry of intercession went up from the hill of Ramah for that wayward king whom he so dearly loved (xv. 34, 35). Don't you think it must be a faint reflection of the pain in God's heart when any of us goes from Him into evil.

(*At beginning or end of this lesson read 1 Samuel, parts of chap. ix., xi., xiv., xv.*)

QUESTIONS FOR LESSON I

Why should this study of Jewish history be of any more value than that of any other history?

How did Saul first meet Samuel?

Describe his election and coronation.

Tell some of his acts of disobedience.

What is your opinion about the slaughter of the Amalekites?

LESSON II

SAUL'S GLOOMY END

The portions referred to.

Also parts of 1 Samuel XXVIII., XXXI.

§ 1. An Evil Spirit from the Lord

Do you think you could put into words, now, the chief lesson of King Saul's life? Try to make pupils express it in their own words—that young people may start with many good gifts of God, position, opportunities, endowments, attractive gifts of body and mind—even with good desires, and aspirations, the gift of God's Holy Spirit to bless them—and yet that they may spoil their lives utterly, why? Because there is something in the inner shrine and centre of each one's being that belongs to one's own self, something at the centre of the will that God Himself will not overrule or force. We must each for himself surrender our own hearts to God. And if we do not God has to wait and wait, and see His good gifts wasted, and see us suffering failure and sorrow, and remorse and pain, until at last some day—perhaps when the boys and girls have grown to be dissatisfied men and women—some day they find out that their life is a big mistake, and that the love of the Father has been waiting all the time, and so perhaps their hearts are touched at last to cry to Him, "Lord, whom have I in heaven but Thee, and there is none on earth that I desire in comparison of Thee."

In this life, at any rate, Saul never got thus far, and so his life was spoiled. We read in the last chapter that he had drifted so far from God's life-plan for him that Samuel had to denounce on him the stern anger of God, and warn him that another should take his place as king. This was the severest blow of Saul's life. And the sad thing in it is that it led to no repentance, no sorrow for having disappointed God.[1] What one sees is rather bitterness, and peevishness, and a feeling of being ill-treated, and, later on, a jealous watching for the rival who should displace him. From this time forward we see him growing sullen and gloomy and suspicious— sometimes even violent.

See chapter xvi. 14. "The Spirit of the Lord departed from Saul, and an evil spirit from the Lord troubled him." Do you think that same thing happens to men now? Yes, just the same. A man's sins harden his heart, and close up as it were the avenues through which the Holy Spirit helps men. Then comes the misery of conscience tormenting him, and, because he won't

[1]Chapter xv. 24 may seem to contradict this. But I think he was only sorry for what he had lost, and in the 30th verse it would seem that he only wanted Samuel to turn and worship with him in order that he should not be dishonoured before the army.

29

obey it, darkening his life with remorse, and making his future full of weariness and troubled apprehension. Do you think it strange to call it an evil spirit from the Lord? I think anything that torments us, and frightens us, and keeps us from resting in our sins, is from the Lord; even the horrible *delirium tremens* that comes on a drunkard, and terrifies him with the horrors of hell here on earth.

§ 2. Jealousy

Now David comes into Saul's life. But we shall have David's story afterwards. At present I want to keep your attention on Saul, and shall refer to David only when necessary for this purpose.

David first meets the king after the fight with Goliath of Gath (*ch.* xvii.), where already you see Saul was beginning to show his gloom and despondency (*v.* 11). Saul at first took a great fancy to the boy, and made him his armour-bearer, little knowing what was in the future, and David's harp was a great comfort to the king when his black fits of temper and despondency were on him. David rose in military life from post to post till he became a famous captain (*ch.* xviii.) and won victory and glory, and the enthusiasm of the people. Then Saul grew jealous, remembering the old days when all shouted in enthusiasm for himself. Then one unfortunate day, as David returned from a victorious expedition against the Philistines,[1] the king overheard the song of victory, and unluckily caught the words

---

[1] Not the Goliath battle. See the Revised Version.

of the song "Saul hath slain his thousands but David his ten thousands." He was very angry. One does not wonder. Then I think it was that the keen suspicion first flashed on him. "Could this be the threatened rival to the throne?" "What can he have more but the kingdom?" cries the jealous king. "And Saul eyed David from that day forward." (*ch*. xviii. 6-9).

From that day he grew still more fierce and gloomy. Gradually the brooding gloom and ill-temper grew into violence—into a sort of semi-insanity that darkened his later life. It is awful to see how evil tempers grow towards madness. I have known people going on with peevishness and ill-temper till they grew half mad. Look at Saul (*vv.* 10, 11). On the morrow in his rage he flung a javelin at David. Then (*v.* 12) he grew afraid of David because the Lord was with him, and the people loved him. Then his elder daughter Merab was to marry David, and Saul gave her to another. Then his younger daughter Michal fell in love with David, and Saul first tried by a trick to get him killed by the Philistines (xviii. 22), and then (xix. 11) laid an ambush to murder him in his house with his young wife. It is perfectly awful to see how rapidly Saul fell. One hopes that, perhaps, he was only partly to blame, that perhaps this semi-madness might partly excuse him. It is hard to distinguish the border-line between fierce ill-temper and madness. One grows into the other.

David had to flee for his life (xix. 18). The priests at Nob were kind to him (*ch*. xxi.), but Doeg, Saul's body-servant, the man it is said who was with him when seeking his asses, saw this and reported the priests to Saul (xxii. 9), and the cruel, half mad king commanded Doeg to slaughter them. Then began the long persecution of David when year after year Saul's soldiers hunted him over mountain and desert to take his life. All this we shall learn more fully in the Story of David.

Ah! poor, foolish, mad, wicked Saul who had cast away God's good gifts! And yet he was not all bad. It is so touching to see the good in the man struggling with the evil. Again the Spirit of the Lord came upon him as he was chasing David, as if to show that God never gives a man up, and he returned quiet and subdued for a while. Then twice over we read of days when he lay in David's power, and David refused to hurt him—once when he lay asleep and David stole down to him and carried off his spear—once when he came into the dark cave, and David cut off his robe, but did not hurt him. And it is touching to see how the king's hardening heart was touched, and the old generous heart showed itself again. "Is it thy voice, my son David, return to me, I have sinned, I have played the fool." And he lifted up his voice and wept (*ch.* xxiv. 16). But in a few days he was as bad as ever.

Remember, young people, that all this is happening in the same way to-day. A man's life is growing worse. The better nature is being slowly destroyed. Yet it keeps at times flashing out like this. And these flashes of good are God's reminders of His high purpose for the man. They are showing him what he might be; what God wants him to be. Ah! if Saul would but turn and obey

God still! It was such a pity! He had so much of the generous and good in him. But he spoiled it all.

§ 3. Unhappy Old Age

Now we are drawing near the end. The clouds are setting black and heavy in the evening of his life on this poor, wicked, wayward king who had sinned away his opportunities. God has rejected him, the people are losing trust in him, his best friends have fled from him, David, the friend of his early days, is hiding from him. Samuel, who mourned for him, has been two years in his grave. He is alone except for Jonathan, the brave, unselfish son who watched over him always. And remorse for all his evil is strong within him. Life has grown very dreary for Saul, as it usually does in advancing years for every irreligious man.

Young people, be sure that this is so. You may be gay enough in your bright young days without religion. But you can't go on thus as you grow old. You can only pretend. Thank God for that. He will not let us be happy away from Him. He has made us for himself, and if we persist in doing without Him we must be dissatisfied and unhappy in older years. The Devil has no happy old people.

Many troubles were coming on Saul. He had been a great warrior. He had inspired high enthusiasm in his soldiers and deep dread in his enemies, But as he grew older, his powers failed. The enthusiasm and the dread died down. The enemies whom he once scattered began to close in on him like dogs on a dying stag.

The Philistines from the five towns are advancing in a combined movement. Saul is on Mount Gilboa with his army, a dispirited army because led by a dispirited king. Two hundred years ago Gideon had gathered his little troop on that same field, and by his daring and enthusiasm for God and right had swept the Midianite raiders from the land. But there was no Gideon now, Saul had lost heart; "when he saw the camp of the Philistines he was afraid and his heart trembled exceedingly." Not that he was a coward. No, but he had lost heart. The evil tempers indulged had filled his life with gloom. He knew not where to turn. The spirit of the Lord had departed from him, and when he inquired of the Lord the Lord answered him not.

§ 4. *The Witch of Endor*

And then a strange thing happened. Yet not strange, just what happens to-day also. The man who has lost his religion often turns with credulity to some grotesque superstition. It is a curious thing. But I think it is a sort of punishment. Our souls are made for God and His teaching, and if we will not let the soul have that it will often seek some foolish imitation to satisfy itself.

So with Saul. In his earlier days he had destroyed the witches out of the land. But away in one of the half-heathen corners of the land there still lived one of them, the "Witch of Endor" she was called. In the dead of night as she pursued her incantations, three mysterious visitors came to her cabin, cloaked and disguised. One of them, the chief, was tall and kingly. His face was hidden in his cloak. The witch watches him sharply. "Call up for me," he asks, "from the land beyond the grave, Samuel the Prophet!"

I have no intention here of discussing the question of Modern Spiritualism as to whether it is possible to communicate with the spirits departed. I believe we have hints in the Bible that our dear ones departed know about us (*e.g.* Hebrews xii. 1). I think they watch over us and help us, and probably in the mysterious Paradise Land win blessings for us by their prayers. I think the spirit world is all around us much nearer than we think. If I were ever offered clear evidence I should see no difficulty in believing that they could communicate with us.

I can only say that in passing. However, in this case, whether it was a special miracle or not, you cannot doubt that the historian, at any rate, believed in a real coming of Samuel. I don't think it was Saul's great longing that brought him. If that could bring them—ah! they would often come to us. It is all mysterious. But just as the Bible says (Luke ix. 30) that Moses and Elias came out of the great Waiting Life to stand with our Lord on the Mount of Transfiguration and talk of His decease which he should accomplish at Jerusalem, so too, I think, the Bible means to say that Samuel came. It ought not to seem so strange. The strange thing to me is that they are not always breaking through into our world when they must know that our hearts are longing for knowledge of them. But God knows best why they do not come.

Is not it very sad to see poor Saul turning to witches for knowledge after forsaking God? And is it not very touching to see him in his sore extremity turn to the one true friend of his youth for comfort, to hear him pleading with Samuel in his lonely misery. "I am sore distressed," he cries, "for the Philistines make war on me, and God is departed from me and answereth me no more." It nearly brings tears into one's eyes to hear him.

But there seems no cry of repentance—only of deep gloom and misery. And from the Unseen Land the old prophet repeats and deepens the doom: "The Lord shall deliver Israel into the hand of the Philistines, and tomorrow shalt thou and thy sons be with me" in the world of the departed. Then Saul fell straightway all along the earth and was sore afraid because of the words of Samuel, and there was no strength left in him.

§ 5. *Gilboa*

Not much help in that awful night to nerve him for to-morrow's battle. Do you remember Richard III. the night before Bosworth Field, as the ghosts of the dead came to him in his dreams to remind him of his evil deeds and threaten to "sit heavy on his sword to-morrow." So was the night before Gilboa to the doomed Saul.

This is the last scene in our story of Saul—the last glimpse of him ere the fast gathering darkness settles on him for ever. It is the evening of the battle. The Israelites are flying in all directions before the victorious foe, and the grim old warrior king is standing alone. The crown is on his head, the royal bracelet on his arm. He is leaning on his great battle spear—leaning heavily, for he has received his death-wound. The battle is lost. Jonathan, the thoughtful, loving son who never left him, is lying dead before him, with his two brothers at his side. What is there left to live for any more? So the weary old king "took his sword and fell upon it and he died." And there was no royal funeral, no "Dead March in Saul" to thrill men at his grave. There he lay neglected on the hill side till the Philistines found him and nailed up his body in their idol temple.

That was the end. A gloomy end. He had spoiled his life, wasted his opportunities, forsaken his God. Who would have predicted such a fate thirty years before when he stood forth on his Coronation Day amid the shouts of an enthusiastic people? O young people, life is very solemn for us all, and no man can waste and spoil it without an awful reckoning time. We have nothing to do with his final fate. St. Bernard and others of old declared that he was eternally lost. We must not be wise above what is written. Even without that his fate is awful enough, the fate to which the stern love of God sends every impenitent man when he dies, for the man's own good you may be sure. The judgment of Saul is still in the future, and "to the Lord our God belong mercies and forgiveness though we have rebelled against Him."

(Read portions referred to above.)

QUESTIONS FOR LESSON II

What first roused Saul's jealousy against David?

How did he show it?

Was Saul entirely bad? Notice any signs of good in him.

What is the story about the Witch of Endor?

Describe Saul's death.

How do you account for the good in him and how for the evil?

DAVID—HIS YOUTH

1 Samuel XVI. 1-13, XVII.

§ 1. Was His Religion Real?

We have studied the sad lessons of the life of Saul. We begin now the lessons of the life of David. Very different lessons. I don't at all mean that David was an entirely good man, or Saul an entirely bad man. No, they were both men with good and evil in them. But they differed greatly in the attitude of their hearts towards God. The Bible speaks of David with decided approval, and of Saul with decided blame. But you must not therefore think it your duty to look only for good in the one, and for evil in the other. That is not real Bible study. You will miss the best of the Bible teaching unless you are quite honest and candid, giving full weight to the evil and the good in each of its characters.

I don't like troubling you with so much introduction before the story, but I am so much afraid of your making any mistake. I have heard people object that David should be called in Scripture the "man after God's heart."

They think of some grave faults and sins in his life, and they have an uneasy feeling about his beautiful psalms, that they are the utterances of a man whose religion is hardly very practical. They say, "He could say very beautiful prayers, and write very beautiful psalms, but with all this he could do actions that were by no means very beautiful." And it troubles their conscience that God should approve of any man for beautiful beliefs or beautiful prayers. They say, "It is the man's life that ought to count with God." Are they right? Surely they are right. Conscience and Scripture are both from the same God, and unless something is wrong they should correspond with each other. It would be horrible that you should ever learn to think that the Bible encourages any unreal religion, or considers sentimental piety or sentimental beliefs in God any equivalent for a clean, righteous, faithful life. The Bible knows of no righteousness except doing and striving after right.

But what the Bible values is the whole bent and aim of the life. It says, it is the relation to God that matters, that the first and last and supreme duty of every man all his life is to strive after right, to put God first. A man may be silly and stupid, and awkward and unattractive, yet if that aim of his life is right Scripture approves of Him. Even if in some great crisis of temptation he falls into a great sin, the verdict of Scripture does not alter. The man's life aim is still after God. He hates and despises himself and bitterly repents for his sin. He is on God's side still in spite of it.

I think David was a true and real man, longing to be good, longing after God in spite of his sins. His cryings after God are at least as real as yours and mine when we have sinned. We are bitterly ashamed. We have greatly sinned. But that does not make it unreal or hypocritical that we should express our desires for God. We *do* want God really and truly. We would not give Him up for all the world could give us, though we do sin shamefully against Him. Try and judge David as you judge yourself, and perhaps you will learn how, in spite of his sins, this man through the depth of his sorrow and the earnestness of his struggle may have been more after God's heart than many a careless critic who judges him.

§ 2. Boyhood

Now for the story.

Away in the old heroic days of the world, before Romulus and Remus were suckled by the wolf, before Homer wrote about the siege of Troy, there lived amongst the hills of Bethlehem a farmer and weaver of sacred carpets.[1] His name was Jesse. A hundred years earlier the Bible story tells of Ruth, a Moabite girl, who was loved by the rich farmer Boaz. This farmer Jesse was their grandson. Jesse had eight sons and the youngest was David. So you see David had the blood of the Moabite girl in his veins, which I suppose explains why, long after this (*ch.* xxii. 3, 4), he sent his father for shelter to the King of Moab. Perhaps it explains, too, his broader outlook in his Psalms. I don't think he

---

[1] So the Jewish Talmud says.

regarded Jehovah as the God of Israel only, caring not for other nations.

The little David had seven brothers all older than himself, and two sisters or step-sisters oldest of all. These sisters were probably mothers of children before the younger brother David was born, so that David's young nephews were as old as himself. I think of the little boys playing soldiers together, David and Joab, and Amasa and Asahel, and then I think of sad days in their later lives when they played soldiers in earnest. Sometimes if little boys could see the later life it might spoil a good deal of the play.

I don't think David was of much account in the family. He was the sheep-boy away out on the pasture fields all the day long. But he was of much account in God's plan for the world. God was preparing him for great things by-and-by. It is very wonderful that mystery of God's preparation of the men who are to help Him by-and-by in putting the poor world straight, the silent influences playing around them all unconsciously to themselves. That is what makes the story of a great man's childhood so interesting.

Look at this boy, the bright, handsome, ruddy, young shepherd, all unconsciously educating himself for his great future. Not merely for being King of Israel—that was but a small thing—but for being the great inspired Psalmist who for 3,000 years past has helped the world more than any other man. He did not know that God was training him, but He was. His bodily powers were braced by the hardy open-air life, his courage and self-reliance brought out by dangers to his flock. Then the solitariness of the long day, the absence of distracting cares and excitements encouraged reflection and quiet thought. I have been reading lately about a little shepherd boy on the Welsh hills wondering and thinking all day long while the genius of a great sculptor was growing within him. So with David. All day long practising with his harp, singing to his sheep, thinking in his solitary life those strange, deep thoughts that come to lonely boys. And all the time, though he did not know it, by these thoughts and deeds God was preparing him to be one of the world's greatest helpers.

God is doing the same thing to-day, preparing children for some life plan that He has for them. I often watch with wonder the young minds growing, and wonder what God is training them for.

§ 3. God's Call

Then, at last, one day in God's good time, his call came. A hurried messenger running to the pastures, "Samuel the great prophet is at the sacrifice and has sent for you." Away he goes. And when Samuel saw him come all flushed with running and excitement, the heart of the old prophet went out to him at once as it had gone out long ago to the young Saul who had failed him. The Divine impulse moved him to lay hands on the lad, to pour the holy oil on his head, to whisper to him so that no one else could hear, "God anoints thee king." "And the Spirit of the Lord," it says, "came mightily upon David from that day forward." Just as He had come to Saul.

I suppose in all the after memories of the lad that was the supreme day of his life. There are certain days like that in many of our lives, days that we look back on as being more important than all the days before. Then David went back to his sheep with the dangerous secret locked in his heart. It would be death to his family and ruin to Bethlehem if Saul suspected it. So the boy went back to his old work.

But how different life must have seemed to him now. How fast his mind would grow. Think of him wandering through the pastures hearing ever in his ears the whisper of the prophet, "God anoints thee king." How it would bring the wonder into his heart and the far-off look into his eyes as he thought of God's great life plan for him. Ah, that is what would make all boys grow high and noble—the conviction that God had a life plan for them. And He has, I think, for each of you as well as for David.

§ 4. *The Spirit of the Lord*

And then the Spirit of the Lord that came mightily upon him at his anointing! How solemn that would make the days that followed! How would it affect him? As it affects all men. High hopes and aspirations, new powers awaking—all the baser side of him more subdued—all the desires after God, all the awe and wonder and sense of God's presence deepened.

Let me repeat again that you must not think of this as some great miracle of Bible times. That gift is much commoner than men think to-day. It would be more common still if people would but crave for it. The feeling that comes to the girl at her first Communion, the resolves of the young student on his Ordination Day comes from God's Spirit. And, do you know, I think God's Spirit is teaching even careless people who do not pray for it at all. When I see a thoughtless young mother with her first little baby in her arms feeling the whirl of new strange impulses and desires about the child, I think, like as on David, the Spirit of the Lord comes mightily upon her, and she learns what love means, and how deep are the depths of self-sacrifice. She finds out wonderingly that she would give her life for that child's life—her heaven, if possible, for that child's heaven. And, perhaps, thus she learns the meaning of God's love and God's self-sacrifice, that what she would do for her child by the necessity of her motherhood, God must do for all of us by the necessity of His fatherhood. Remember in such simple common ways may come the Spirit of the Lord.

So, I suppose, God's Spirit came to David and showed him, as it shows that mother, deeper things than he ever saw before. In the morning as he led out his sheep to the green pastures he would learn to think that his care for the sheep was a little parable of God's care for him and he would feel:

> "The Lord is my Shepherd. I shall not want.
> He maketh me to lie down in green pastures," etc.
> —Psalm xxiii.

45

As he looked out into the glorious eastern dawn God would seem to him visibly present, and he would sing:

"The heavens declare the glory of God,
   The firmament showeth His handiwork."
"The sun cometh forth as a giant out of His chamber," etc.
                                    —Psalm xix.

I suppose it is at this great crisis of his life when "the Spirit of God came mightily upon him," that the keynote of his whole life was struck. All through his life, all through his psalms, that note is ringing. What is it? This. *That God was close to him and took an interest in him and had a life purpose for him. That he was weak and helpless without God. That he could do anything by the help of God.*

Think of the power it was in that boy's life to feel God thus standing about him. Look at him when he had faced the lion and the bear. "The Lord delivered me from the lion and the bear." Don't you think a lad like that would be ready now to face Goliath?

§ 5. David and Goliath

Soon after his father sends him one day to the camp with a message to his brothers. A strange sight it is that meets his eye.

It is the battle-field of the Valley of Elah. The camp of Israel is on one slope, the big tents of the Philistines on the other. The Israelites are rather small men, lithe and clever. The Philistines are big men; big, stupid,

46

thick-headed giants, the same as when Samson used to fool them and laugh at them long ago. There is great excitement on both sides. And David watches and listens wonderingly. Goliath of Gath, their champion, is swaggering in the Philistine lines, "defying the armies of the living God," challenging any man to come across and fight him. And all Israel stands cowed and silent before him. King Saul is in his tent moody and despondent. There was a day when he would have made short work of Goliath. But that day was past. The Spirit of the Lord was departed from him. He will not go. Nobody will go. The whole camp seems to have lost faith in God, and to have sunk into a fog of torpor and despair. Suddenly, like a fresh mountain breeze scattering the fog, comes the shepherd lad's frank, simple faith in God. David cannot understand this cowardice if God is so near. If one is on God's side, he thinks, one could fight anybody. The whole issue of this campaign was turned by this lad's faith in God. Not in himself, or his courage, or his skill. No. He is but a modest shepherd lad with only a sling and a stone. But he trusted, he said, in the might of the living God. If nobody else will fight the giant, said David, I will. "Nay," said King Saul, "thou art but a lad." This was the reply:—"The Lord who delivered me out of the paw of the lion and the bear will deliver me out of the hand of this Philistine." That ended the objections. "Go," said the king, "and the Lord be with thee!"

Of course the whole camp turned out to watch this strange young champion with the empty sling in his hand, and the deep faith in God in his heart. It did them all good to feel the contagion of such faith.

Down the slope they watch him to the stream in mid-valley. They see him choose his stones carefully, and then walk on. The Israelites are not a humorous race, but it must have been amusing to watch the attitude of the great giant standing in his full armour utterly thunderstruck as it dawns on him that this unarmed boy is being sent out to fight him. How dare they offer such an insult to the greatest warrior of Gath! "And the Philistine cursed David by his gods." Then said David, "Thou comest to me with a sword and spear. I come to thee in the name of the Lord of Hosts. The battle is the Lord's." Ah, how the two armies held their breath now as they watched. It was over in a moment. The raging Philistine rushed at David. David, undaunted, rushed at him. The sharp stone left the sling with unerring aim and lodged itself deep in the brain of Goliath. Oh! what a shout of wonder and triumph rang through the camp of Israel. And David ran and stood on the Philistine, and in a moment he had faced the shouting host with the head of the dead giant in his hand!

This is the thought in my mind as I watch him:— What a training that boy must have got in his religion! What a glorious reality God was in his life! It is humiliating for us in the full light of Christianity that many of us are so far behind that Old Testament boy. But it is a grand lesson of the power that consists not in armour and strength, the power that comes to a man who believes that he is nothing, and puts his trust in the might of the living God. You too will have your giants to fight. You have them in some measure now, the fear of your comrades' opinions—the strength of your many temptations. Don't be afraid of them. Trust in God. David was a great man in God's scheme for the world, and that simple trust in God was the secret of his greatness. All through his life it was the same. Look at him before the lion and the bear—look at him before Goliath. Hear him in his later wars: "God teacheth my hand to war, and my fingers to fight. My hope and my refuge, my fortress and deliverer," etc. (Psalm cxliv. 1). Hear him in the 57th Psalm said to be written when fleeing from Saul. "Be merciful unto me, O God, for my soul trusteth in thee. Under thy wings shall be my refuge till this tyranny be overpast." Hear him in the deep despondency of his life. "Why art thou cast down, O my soul, and why art thou disquieted within me? Trust thou in God, for I shall yet praise Him, the help of my countenance and my God." (Psalm xlii. 5).

This is the end of David's young days, his happiest days!

(Read the necessary parts of 1 Samuel xvi. and xvii.)

QUESTIONS FOR LESSON III

David did some very wicked things, yet the Bible says he was pleasing to God. Can you explain?

Tell about his boyhood.

When did he first hear that he was to be king?

Tell of his fight with Goliath.

What was the secret of David's courage?

Quote any verse in the Psalms expressing his feeling towards God.

DAVID AND JONATHAN

1 Samuel XVIII. 1, XX., XXI., etc., XXIII. 14-19;

2 Samuel 1

§ 1. *The Border Line*

There is a border line between boyhood and manhood, between girlhood and womanhood, that young people must all pass one day, and perhaps will sometimes look back regretfully over that line. David passed it that day on the battle-field of Elah. On that day he made acquaintance with the king, he was received into the palace; the old life of the shepherd boy was over for ever.

On that day, too, he made acquaintance with some one else. You remember the scene. The blustering giant, the frightened Israelites, the moody, despondent king. Saul had lost heart, lost trust in God. He would not fight the giant, and probably would not let any one else fight him. Perhaps the earlier stages of that half-insane gloom and passion of his later life had come on him. Perhaps that is why we see beside him, for the first time, in his tent the young prince Jonathan, who all through the after story is ever by his side till they both lie dead together on the field of Gilboa. Perhaps that, too, was why he would not let Jonathan fight the giant. Jonathan had already won his spurs in that daring expedition (*ch.* xiv.) when he and his young armour-bearer alone climbed the enemy's fort and left twenty dead Philistines lying "within half a furrow's length in an acre of land." I fancy that the morbid despondency of the king made him afraid to let Jonathan go, and that Jonathan had to stand idly by, chafing and longing fiercely for some champion to wipe out the disgrace from Israel.

I picture him to myself thus chafing when the groups outside began to talk excitedly, and the shepherd lad was brought to the king's tent. At once the prince's attention is fixed on him. This lad actually believes in God's close presence. He is actually going to fight the giant! You can imagine how Jonathan listened, how he watched the fight, how his heart swelled within him at the shout of the people when the huge Philistine lay dead upon the ground. Don't you think there was something very fine in that young warrior rejoicing that another should do the deed which he himself could not do? It is only great souls who can feel like that. And then when David came back with Goliath's head, and he heard his simple modest replies to the king, the charm deepened. Further talk that evening showed him more of the lad's beautiful nature until we read "the soul of

Jonathan was knit unto the soul of David, and he loved him as his own soul."

§ 2. Friendship

That is the beginning of one of the most beautiful friendships in history. I don't know why some friendships are sudden like that. There was much to attract these two—they were both young—most of our friendships are made when we are young—both a bit lonely at home—both brave—both modest—and, best of all, both truly religious. I don't believe the truest, highest friendships are ever to be had without God in them.

There was also in these two another element in great friendships. They were each great-minded enough to love and admire the superiority of the other. Poor mean creatures that like to belittle and detract from men greater than themselves can never make a deep friendship. David of course knew of Jonathan's daring deeds. Jonathan had looked now on what seemed a more daring deed than his own. And they could each admire and look up to each other. Nay, I think they could do more. They could each idealize the other and see him better than he was. I am sure Jonathan thought more of David than he deserved. And so did David of Jonathan. It is so with all beautiful friendships. People say that love is blind. Yes, thank God, in that sense it is. And it is good for us. There are some of us who feel honestly ashamed at times as we see what our dearest think of us. We know it is not true. We feel at times inclined to undeceive them. Better not. The best thing is not to break down their ideals, but to try for very shame's sake to be what they think we are.

Seek the gift of deep true friendships in your lives; I sometimes think that people are getting too busy and too fussy now for deep, true friendships. We make many acquaintances, nice people whom we nod to in the street and ask to gatherings at our homes—many acquaintances, but I don't think so many friends as people in quieter ages of the world made—the sort of friends who have the key to that little side door in our heart that admits into the secret rooms of life.

And seek friends that you can admire and look up to. Not the poor sort that flatter you and degrade you. Seek friends nobler than yourself, who will help to keep you up to what is honourable and good. Especially try to get friends religious in the true sense, not goody-goody talkers about religion. Get God into your friendships if you can, that they may last for ever.

§ 3. *Parting*

That is the first scene in this friendship. The battlefield of Elah. The second is a year later in the king's dining-hall (1 Samuel xx. 24, etc.). King Saul is at the table moody and distraught. Abner is beside him, the captain of the host; Prince Jonathan is opposite anxiously watching the face of his father as the gloom deepens on it. And it is easy to see there is constraint and embarrassment on them all.

David's place is empty. The meaning is this. For some time past there has been trouble in the air, David and Jonathan had had many months of companionship, but it would seem as if the end were near. David had risen very high and very fast since the victory over Goliath. In a few months he had won the king's favour, the friendship of Jonathan, the hand of the princess Michal, the love and the enthusiasm of the people. "All Israel loved him, and he was greatly set by." A high place indeed for the poor shepherd lad. But high places are dangerous places. Kings whose power rests on military success cannot safely have popular favourites too near to the throne. So Saul became jealous. The trouble began with the tactless cry of the maidens, "Saul hath slain his thousands, but David his ten thousands." Saul became fiercely angry, then he became suspicious. Is this the rival threatened by Samuel? What can he have more but the kingdom? One day he flung a javelin at him. Another day he conspired to murder him. And every failure made him more determined, till at last he spoke openly of killing him. So David had to hide.

For two days past the king with irritation had marked his vacant place. Now the evil spirit of rage is rising, and he turns fiercely to David's friend. "Why cometh not the son of Jesse to meat?" Jonathan explained. The king grew fiercer, and spoke cruelly. Then Jonathan stood up in defence of his friend. Eagerly he pleaded for him. Boldly he recounted his good deeds. Fearlessly he challenged the justice of the king in ill-treating a man who had done no wrong. His answer was the spear of the king, flung at him, and a coarse, brutal gibe about some shame of his mother, that we don't know of. "Jonathan arose from the table in fierce anger." But before he left Saul launched his parting taunt. "As long as the son of Jesse liveth on the ground thou shalt never be established in thy kingdom." Ah! it was a black, bitter day for Jonathan, the spear, the coarse taunt about his mother, but deeper than all the clear conviction that he and his friend must say good-bye for ever.

I wonder if there is any finer character in history than the princely friend of David. What a great King of Israel he would have made, if God had not needed him for greater things in the Unseen Land! See him not merely standing up for his absent friend at the risk of his life, but actually consenting to be deprived of the kingdom. "Thou shalt be king, and I shall be next unto thee." (1 Samuel xxiii. 17).

All that night he had to brace himself for the parting, and next morning he went out to shoot the arrows (xx. 35), the prearranged signal to David that he should flee the court. Ah! it is very touching. Only two verses (*vv.* 41, 42) record the keen, agonized parting, how "they kissed one another, and wept with one another, and David exceeded." "Then David arose, and departed, and Jonathan went unto the city." So they parted—to meet no more on earth except for one brief stolen interview in the after years (*ch.* xxiii. 16, etc.).

§ 4. *The Friends Who Strengthen Us*

Again the scene changes. It is midnight in the forest of Ziph. David is a hunted outlaw with a price upon his head. And through the trees in the midnight Jonathan is stealing up to his friend from the camp of the king. For what? To "strengthen his hands in God." Is not that a beautiful office to do for one's friend? And it is only friends like Jonathan that can really do it.

Ever since the "Day of the Arrows" they have been in opposite camps. David, an outlaw fleeing for his life, Jonathan in the camp of the king, who was pursuing him. And yet as you read the story you feel that Jonathan was right, and also that David saw that he was right. Stronger than these ties of attachment to his friend were the ties of duty of sonship, of loyalty to the king, of care for that poor, passionate, half-mad father whom he dares not leave. It was bitterly hard. Yes. But it was right. And Jonathan elected to do the right at any cost. His father might sneer at him, gibe at him about his mother, torture him about his friend—never mind. His duty was there. And both he and David knew it.

Ah! thank God for the friendships that are kept thus pure and high, that even for friend or lover will not swerve from the right. Remember you owe it to your friend to keep for him always your best self. Not even for his sake must you lower your ideals. Nay, all the more for his sake you must keep them high. One reads some times of a friend doing a mean thing to help his friend or of a girl leaving pressing home duties to marry her lover. Ah! it is a pity that the beautiful high thing, God's good gift of love, should be thus besmeared. The whole quality of it becomes lowered. The whole enjoyment of each other becomes spoiled.

Because Jonathan would not thus degrade his friendship he is able now, stealing up through the forest, to "strengthen his friend's hands in God." Ah! may God give you friends who will do that for you! May He enable you to do that for your friend. For, be you sure of this, the deepest, truest friendship can never be had without religion. There are many friendships of kindly generous people who would do much for each other but are unable to do the best. They have never shared deep high thoughts together about nobleness of life here, about unselfish service hereafter. They have never prayed for each other, nor strengthened each other's hands in God. I don't suggest mere pious talking. Not so much talking but being. David and Jonathan were the better men for their friendship. So should be you and your friend. I wonder, if Jonathan had remained to strengthen the hand of David, would David have ever fallen into the great sin of his life.

§ 5. Jonathan Is Dead!

Five years have elapsed. It is an anxious day for Israel. David is up in the rocks of Ziklag waiting for news. His band of outlaws are standing round him peering out into the valley. They are waiting. All Israel is waiting for tidings from the camp. For the Philistines have swarmed in from their five towns, and Saul with his army is surrounded at Gilboa. So David waits and watches. He knows that the result of this expected battle will decide much for the nation and much for himself. He knows, too, that Jonathan is on the battle-field with the king, Jonathan whom he has never seen since that night in the wood.

So all that long day David thought of his friend, and watched and waited and surely prayed for him. Now the watchers have sprung to their feet. A flying messenger from Gilboa! "The battle is lost, the army is routed— *and Saul and Jonathan his son are dead also!*" Jonathan is dead also! Jonathan is dead also! Do you know how a phrase like that keeps vibrating in one's brain? Ah! that would hit David hardest of all. The others would think of defeat, of national disgrace, David would think chiefly of that brave, sad face upturned to the sky on that distant battle-field. "O, I am distressed for thee, my brother Jonathan! Very pleasant hast thou been to me. Thy love for me was wonderful, passing the love of women."

There is one great comfort. He has none but noble memories of his dead friend. True to the last! He had done the right. He had guarded his father. He had fought by his side. He had fallen at his feet. Pierced by Philistine spears, the brave true heart had gone back to God, and Israel was sorely the poorer for the loss of Jonathan. Please God your friends will have such memories of you when you die. It is the greatest comfort in any bereavement.

§ 6. *Friendships in the Hereafter*

Do you think we are done now with the story of that beautiful friendship? Ah, no! The scene changes once more. But I have not the materials to paint the next picture for you. The grass had been twenty-five years growing over the bones of Prince Jonathan when a weary old King of Israel laid down his poor soiled life and passed into the Unseen Land—and the two friends were together again. I cannot depict that meeting for you. I can only dimly imagine the delight of it. I can only vaguely guess that God helped the poor fallen king by the old friend's friendship again. But one thing I know is true beyond imagining and guessing—that the two friends *were* together again—*are* together again in God's everlasting Kingdom to-day.

Do you ask, "How could one tell that they would meet—that they would know each other?" There was only One who ever lived on earth that could answer that question and he answered it. He had made a new friend as He lay dying on the Cross—a poor, humble, penitent friend who could not bear to lose touch with Him ever again. "Lord, don't forget me," he cried, "remember me when Thou comest in Thy Kingdom." And that tenderest of all friends reassured him. "To-day we shall meet. To-day thou shalt be with me." Surely He meant to imply, "To-night, when our dead bodies hang stiff upon the Cross, we two shall know each other in the Unseen Land as the two who hung upon the Cross together."

I think that is a hint from which we may gather much. Therefore don't talk of David's and Jonathan's friendship in the past tense. Not that they *were* friends— but they *are* friends to-day, growing doubtless closer to God and closer to each other through all the ages of eternity. Therefore we must cherish our friendships, cherish our loves. Keep them always true and high.

Keep God in them. For every true friendship and every true love that has the nature of God in it will go on for ever and ever.

(Read 1 Samuel xviii. 1, xx. 24, etc., xxiii. 14-19; 2 Samuel i.)

QUESTIONS FOR LESSON IV

What chiefly is the teaching of this lesson?

What do you think of Jonathan? Why?

Tell of his first meeting with David.

What sort of friends should we seek and what should we try to do for them?

Tell some things that Jonathan did for his friend.

Where did Jonathan die? Was that the end of that friendship?

THE OUTLAW

1 Samuel XXI. and the necessary parts of
XXII., XXIII., XXIV. and 2 Samuel I.

We have dealt with two sections of David's story:
(1) His youth and preparation for his great future;
(2) The story of his friendship with Jonathan. Now we
come to tell more fully of his life as an outlaw, hunted
for years over mountain and desert like "bonnie Prince
Charlie," in the Highlands 150 years ago, only that his
outlaw period was only a few months; while David's
extended to several years. It was a time of much strain
and trouble and left a deep impress on his life, and it
would appear in his psalms also. If we may judge by
their titles, and also by their tone, several psalms may
be marked off as "Songs of the Outlaw." We shall find
them as we go on.

§ 1. *The Outlaw's Faith*

You remember how, in the midst of David's sudden

prosperity at court, the anger and jealousy of Saul broke out against him. You remember how it was first roused by the tactless war song, "Saul hath slain his thousands, but David his ten thousands." Then came the keen suspicion, growing at last into certainty, that David was in God's providence to become king. Then came the flinging of the javelin and the plot to murder him at his house, and the open discussion at the royal table about the political necessity of his death. Then Jonathan warned him by the arrow flight, and David had to fly from wife and home and friends and high position to be an outlaw hiding in the mountain.

Does somebody ask, what about the theory now of God prospering his servant? What about David's faith now when flying for his life? If you read some of the outlaw's songs, ascribed to David and to this time, you will get David's answer. Read Psalm vii.: *"O Lord my God, in Thee do I put my trust. Save me from all them that persecute me and deliver me."* Read Psalm xi.: *"In the Lord put I my trust, how say ye to my soul that she should flee as a bird to the mountains. For lo, the wicked bend their bow, etc., etc. . . . But the Lord is in His holy temple, The Lord's throne is in Heaven, His eyes behold, His eyelids try the children of men."* I don't think the outlaw life made David at all feel that God had forgotten him. Prosperity may not by any means be always the best thing for us.

At 1 Samuel xxi. the story of the outlaw days begins. Before this he had fled to Samuel (1 Samuel xix. 18) to Naioth in Ramah, a sort of Divinity School for training "the sons of the prophets." Perhaps David had some notion of joining them. But Saul soon chased him thence. Where should he go next? He does not know. He will go to Nob and ask Ahimelech the priest. So he reaches the slopes of the Mount of Olives, and there comes to a very curious and interesting place—a little colony of priests, descendants of Eli, taking charge of—what do you think? The ancient Tabernacle of the Wilderness Wanderings. Fancy seeing the Tabernacle again! Don't you feel as if you were thrown back to the days of Moses? Solitary, hungry, unarmed, he reaches the priestly dwellings. He longs for a piece of the shewbread. The old priest felt that by the law of the church that shewbread is sacred; but he felt too, that, by the higher law of mercy, a starving man must be fed. So he dared to do what brought great trouble on his house, but which also, long centuries afterwards, brought commendation from Christ. "Have ye never read what David did?" says the Lord (St. Matthew xii. 4).

Then as David had no weapon the kindly old priest lifts down the sword of Goliath which hung as a trophy in the Tabernacle like the banners in our cathedrals today. Can't you fancy how the touch of that sword would bring back to David that great deed in the Valley of Elah? But soon he had something else to think of, for, as he girds on the great sword, suddenly his eye rests on a dusky face, keen and malicious, hiding in the background, and with dread in his heart he recognizes Doeg, the Edomite, the most trusty and most dangerous of the servants of Saul. Ah! since Doeg knew him there would be trouble soon for David or for the priests. Doeg would surely tell the king. So David fled with a troubled heart, whither do you think? Actually to Gath, the city of Goliath! It seems such a mad thing to fly to Goliath's city with Goliath's sword at his side. Of course, he was recognized. Soon he heard them whispering that unfortunate war song, "Saul hath slain his thousands, etc." Soon he had to pretend insanity to escape with his life. I am rather amused at the retort of the King of Gath when his servants told him: "Have not I got enough lunatics already about me without bringing another to me." (*ch.* xxi. 15).

Soon came the bad news he feared about Doeg and the priests.

Ah! there was good reason for a troubled heart. For the next picture is of the fierce, gloomy king (xxii. 6) at Ramah under the tamarisk tree with his great war spear in his hand. He is angrily chiding his courtiers, angrily complaining, like Henry II. of England complained of Thomas à Becket, that no one would rid him of this pestilent David. Then comes forth Doeg, the Edomite, to complain of the old priest's kindness to David at Nob. Next day the priests are arrested, and when no one else would carry out the fierce sentence of the king, Doeg himself fell on the defenceless men and smote them down in the royal presence. Just one escaped to tell David of the ruthless deed, and Psalm lii. is described in the title as David's psalm about this deed of Doeg.

> "Thy tongue imagineth wickedness. With lies thou
>   cuttest like a sharp razor.
> Thou hast loved to speak all words that may do hurt,
>   O thou false tongue."

§ 2. *A Captain of Freebooters*

Again David has to flee, this time to the Cave of Adullam on the frontier, the country all alive with the romantic legends about Samson. And here were exciting times and strange arrivals in his camp. One day his old playmates, Joab and Amasa and Asahel came to lead his men. Another day eleven Gadite warriors swam the Jordan at flood to reach him (1 Chronicles xii. 15). Later on came Gad, the young divinity student from Naioth, who remained as his prophet and counsellor in all the after years. It was a curious gathering, and all so enthusiastic for their thief. Do you remember 2 Samuel xxiii. 16, when three of them risked their lives to get him a drink of water out of the well of Bethlehem?

There David lived for a good while a captain of freebooters, in some respects an outlaw like Robin Hood in the old days of Merrie England, only he was not a robber. He harried the Philistines, and he exacted tribute from Israelite farmers such as Nabal, but all the time he was guarding the land of these farmers and striking a blow when he could for the good of Israel. Some people will say that though David in the sheepfolds, meditating about God is a beautiful picture of religion, yet that a captain of freebooters, fighting and cattle-lifting, and demanding his tribute at the point of the sword, does not square with their notion of a religious man. I think they are wrong. It is a valuable lesson that a man in this strange position and those dark times could try to be a good man. There are many types of religious life besides those of the monk and devotee, and I think the Bible is presenting this outlaw still as a true man trying to follow the light and get closer to God. And perhaps these fierce outlaw days were part of God's training for David as well as the early days in the sheep pastures. They taught him, perhaps, to know the troubles of his people, and to bring them as well as himself for refuge to God.

I have been looking at two Psalms, which, by their titles, are referred to this period of his life—the 34th and 57th. If we may trust their titles, how deep will be their interest as expressing the attitude of David just then. Look at the 34th.

> "This poor man cried and the Lord heard him.
> And delivered him out of all his troubles,
> The Angel of the Lord encampeth round them
>   that fear Him,
> And delivereth them.
> The young lions do lack and suffer hunger,
> But they that fear Jehovah shall not want
>   any good thing."

And then (*v.* 11) he seems to address his followers:

> "Come, my children, hearken to me,
> I will teach you the fear of the Lord.
> What man is he that listeth to live and would fain
>   see good days.
> Keep thy tongue from evil and thy lips that they
>   speak no guile,
> Depart from evil and do good, seek peace and ensue it.
> For the eyes of the Lord are over the righteous,
> And His ears are open to their cry."

If we could only know with full certainty the history

of the Psalms, what pictures they would call up. Imagine the tired warriors resting on the rocks and their captain teaching them such true and manly religion. What a light that story of the psalms would be on the story of David and Israel.

§ 3. Returning Good for Evil

Next year we find David (*ch.* xxiii.) starting to drive off the Philistines, and save the men of Keilah, at the risk of his life. And the ungrateful cowards tried to repay him by delivering him to Saul. So he fled to the wilderness of Ziph (*v.* 15).

But the Ziphites also sent messengers to Saul, to betray him. Then he hid in the wood, and it was here that Jonathan crept up to him in the night out of the camp of the king to strengthen his hands in God. It was the last meeting on earth of these two friends. The 54th Psalm is the psalm of this period written, we are told, when the Ziphites sent their message unto Saul:

> "Save me, O God, by thy name.
> And judge me by thy might.
> For strangers are now against me,
> And violent men have sought after my soul.
> They have not set God before them."

When next we find David he is hiding in the cave of Engedi over the Dead Sea. All over the hills are the soldiers of Saul, but David and his men keep closely hidden. During the day, the king blunders into the very cave where they lay. Now, said his men to David, "The

Lord hath delivered thine enemy into thine hand." But David was too good a man, and too fond of the old king, in spite of all his evil. He would not touch Saul's life; but I think he must have enjoyed the fun of creeping softly down and cutting off the flowing skirts of the king. And then we have that pathetic scene, David standing on the rocks and pleading with the king to cease this cruel pursuit. "Why do you listen to men who say I seek to injure you? Behold thy robe and how I have saved thy life to-day. Yet I am like a poor hunted creature. Thou huntest my life to take it." And then he appeals from all false stories to the tribunal of God Himself. "The Lord therefore judge between us, and plead my cause, and deliver me."

The hardening heart of Saul is deeply moved. He is not all bad. He breaks into a passion of tears. "David, David, thou art more righteous than I, for thou hast rendered me good, whereas I have rendered thee evil." How astonished David must have been to find him next year in full chase after him again.

§ 4. End of the Outlaw Days

I have only been able to select a few specimen pictures in all these troubled years, and to select a few specimens of the songs of the outlaw.

Now comes the end of the outlaw days. It was the year of Israel's great defeat at Gilboa, and David was in Zildag listening, as all Israel was listening, for news of the war. It would mean a great deal to him. God had spared him all these hard years. What did God mean for him now? If Saul was slain, was he to be king? You know the result: the death of Saul and Jonathan described in our last chapter, the anointing of David in Hebron as king.

Yes, the outlaw days were ended. But the faith of the outlaw days remained. It was still God that he thinks of first (2 Samuel *v.* 12). "And David perceived that *the Lord had established him king over Israel*, and had exalted his kingdom for Israel's sake."

It was the Lord who had made him king, and not for his own sake, or his own reward, but for Israel's sake, because God would lay upon him now that service of his brethren for which all his previous life in the sheepfolds and the mountain caves had been a preparation. Ah! if all kings and merchants, and doctors and clergy, and workers of every kind in the world for God, could take up their work with such faith and unselfishness as that!

(Read 1 Samuel xxi., the necessary parts of ch. xxii., xxiii., xxiv.; 2 Samuel i.)

QUESTIONS FOR LESSON V

Does God always give a good man earthly prosperity? What does He give instead?

Show that David in his hard outlaw life did not forget God or think God had forgotten him.

What do you know of Doeg the Edomite?

Show that David believed it was not chance but God that had made him king.

Show David returning good for evil.

LESSON VI

DAVID AS KING

2 Samuel II. 1-8; III. 32-36; V. 1-12.

Psalm xxiv.   Glance over 1 Chronicles xv.

§ 1. Waiting for the Kingdom

We have now come to the Second Book of Samuel.

Our last chapter closed the story of the outlaw life. Saul was dead. Jonathan was dead. The throne was vacant, and all over the land men's eyes were turned to David as the new king. With the strong forces gathered around him and the strong feeling in his favour he might easily have crushed the discouraged followers of Saul, who, under the leadership of the heroic Abner, made Ishbosheth king (*ch.* ii. 8). But what did he do? (*ch.* ii. 1). Just what he had done in each crisis of his life—enquired of the Lord, and as a result went to Hebron and waited. Next we read (*v.* 4) that the men of Judah, the southern part of the kingdom, assembled to him at Hebron, and made him their king. It was a poor

71

beggarly bit of a kingdom, not half of the full kingdom to which God by Samuel's hand had anointed him long ago. For seven years more he had to wait for that. But he did wait. He had already learned that such things don't come by chance, that God is ruling men's lives. So he waited God's time.

Don't you like his attitude while waiting? (*ch.* ii. 4-8). He hears of the generous daring of the men of Jabesh. You remember how long ago in the beginning of Saul's reign, the Ammonites had surrounded Jabesh and demanded the right eyes of the townsmen should be gouged out, and how the young king in his noble rage sent out the "fiery cross" through the land and saved the town. Now comes the beautiful sequel to the story, telling how the men of Jabesh had remembered it all these years, and how, when the Philistines carried off the corpse of Saul from the battlefield and nailed it as a trophy on the wall of Bethshan, the splendid Jabesh men stole down in the night and risked their lives to carry and bury the dead king. Is it not fine to see how David delighted in this love for his old enemy? "Blessed be ye of the Lord . . . and I will requite you for this kindness to your lord."

Look again (iii. 32, etc.). David's brave adversary Abner has been treacherously murdered, and the king is at the funeral mourning as for a friend. And it says "all the people took notice of it, and it pleased them: for whatsoever the king did pleased all the people." (iii. 36).

It is all so beautiful and chivalrous like the acts

of the most perfect Christian knight. So like that one is tempted to forget the degradation of all life at the time, and to ask what great difference did the coming of Christ make? But look at (*ch.* iii. 2, etc.) the list of David's harem with the new wives added on, and you feel at once the whole disgusting life of an Eastern ruler of that day with his palace full of jealous women gathered in to be wives and under-wives to the king. Look even (*v.* 13, etc.) how the lost wife of his early youth, Michal, the daughter of Saul, was carried off and turned into that harem with the rest of that crowd. How could she be happy or good? How could there be religion or happy home life? How could David know anything of that pure holy family life which is such a power in Christian lands to-day? Don't be surprised then if David sometimes did what good men in our day would not do. And don't forget that was the sort of degraded world to which Christ came to purify and ennoble it.

§ 2. The King's Resolve

Seven years have elapsed. It is David's coronation day. Ishbosheth, Saul's son, is dead. Abner, Saul's general, is dead. The Philistines are growing dangerous, and Israel has no leader. So Israel casts in its lot with Judah, and David is to be king of the whole land. It was a great day for the nation. It is only just mentioned here (*ch.* v.), but the story in 1 Chronicles xii. 23, etc., gives a glorious picture, the lists of the elders and heroes who came, the 3,000 soldiers feasting for three days outside the town.

So, after all these years of patient waiting and many trials and strenuous training, at last David reached the goal which God intended for him, and I want you to see how he felt that it was all of God. Here is his attitude (2 Samuel *v.* 12): "David perceived that the Lord had established him king over Israel for His people Israel's sake." Ah, that is a grand attitude for a king, or ruler, or pastor, or landlord, or employer of labour:—"I am here not by chance, but because this is God's life plan for me, and I am here in this position, not for my own sake, but for my people's sake." The title of Psalm xviii. suggests that it belongs to the period; if so, it gives a wonderful glimpse of David's feelings at this time. And Psalm ci., "a Psalm of David," is set down by most commentators as "The King's resolve": "I will behave myself wisely in a perfect way," "Mine eyes shall be on the faithful of the land that they dwell with me," etc. Read over this Psalm carefully, and think what a grand resolve for the young king.

§ 3. The City of Melchizedek

Now go on with the story (*ch. v.* 6). The new kingdom needs a capital. So David's first exploit is to capture Salem, the old hill fortress of the Jebusites. Think of the interest centred in that town. Even in Abraham's day it was an important fortress. Through its old gates the mysterious Melchizedek, King of Salem, priest of the Most High God, came down in his priestly robe to bless the patriarch. So safe were its fortifications that the besieged laughed at David: "The very blind and lame would be able to keep you out." But Joab and his men climbed the secret precipice path just as Wolfe and his men did at the siege of Quebec, and Salem became Jerusalem, the city of David.

And now, having gained a city for his kingdom, he next resolves that it shall be a Holy City, consecrated by the presence of God. The Ark is to be enthroned in it. You remember the sacred Ark in the time of Moses and Joshua, and the great day when it was carried round the walls of Jericho? It had had strange fortunes since; carried into battle, captured by Philistines, brought back again to Israel, hidden in the woods of Kirjath-jearim. Now David wants it to stand forth before the nation, the visible sign of God's presence, at the centre of his kingdom.

§ 4. *The Coming of the Ark*

I have often tried to picture to myself this "Coming of the Ark." Evidently it was made a great festival day for the nation, and surrounded by all the pomp and all the dramatic setting that David delighted in. The story in 1 Samuel (vi. 12, etc.) suggests this but very slightly. You have to go to the Chronicles, the ecclesiastical history of the nation, for a full glowing description.

1 Chronicles xv. gives the whole procession of priests and Levites, and elders, and captains, and the great white-robed choir of men and boys, the representatives of the whole nation in dramatic procession bringing

up the Ark of God from the woods of Kirjath. "And Chenaniah, the choirmaster, was there with the singers, and they brought up the Ark of the Lord with shouting, and cornets, and trumpets, and cymbals sounding aloud with psalteries and harps." Just glance over this passage—1 Chronicles xv.—to get an idea of the grandeur, and then open your Bible at the 24th Psalm. Read it and keep it open.

Clearly the Psalm is dramatically arranged for some special function, and there is much probability in the belief that it was especially written as one of the Processional Psalms for this Procession of the Ark. Bring the whole dramatic setting before you, see the long line of worshippers winding up the hillside, the Levites in front bearing the Ark. And as they climb up Mount Zion, the Hill of the Lord, a single voice dramatically chants the function:—

> "Who shall ascend unto the hill of the Lord?
> Who shall stand in His holy place?"

To which the great choir responds together:—

> "He that hath clean hands and a pure heart,
> Who hath not lift up his soul unto vanity,
> Nor sworn to deceive his neighbour."

Surely the effect must have been very impressive as the vast crowd winds up the hill. Listen again. They are now at the gate of the old city of Melchizedek, and the Levites are demanding an entrance for the Ark of God:—

> "Lift up your heads, O ye gates,
>   And be ye lift up, ye ancient doors,
>   And the King of Glory shall come in."

But the gates do not open yet. Instead from within the barred city a clear voice rings out—

> "Who is the King of Glory?"

And then you can fancy the delight of King David as he hears the great multitude burst forth in one glad, confident, triumphant cry:—

> "The Lord strong and mighty,
>   The Lord mighty in Battle
>   Even the Lord of Hosts,
>   He is the King of Glory."

And at that proclamation of the Almighty you see the ancient gates crashing back on their hinges and the great procession sweeping through bringing in the Ark of God.

§ 5. *More about David*

There is much more to tell of David as king, but I have not room to tell it. The subduing of all the enemies of Israel till the land had rest. His enthusiastic plans to build a temple, and his disappointment when God forbade him (2 Samuel vii. 5-13). The unselfish spirit that then set him collecting materials exceeding costly for a temple that some one else must have the glory of building. Then the arranging of choirs and psalms, the appointing of Asaph and Heman, and others whose names appear still in the titles of the Psalms.

And then—David's fall. But of this we shall think next day. To-day we close by repeating again the great lesson of the story up to this:—That the glory of David's life consisted in this, that he was a man of faith and prayer. It was his central fixed idea that God was near him, that God would hear him, and that God would help him. It was this "practice of the presence of God" that made him so strong and brave, so calm in adversity, so thoughtful in prosperity. And it is that and that only will do the same for us.

(Read the passages of Scripture referred to above.)

QUESTIONS FOR LESSON VI

What was the fine act of the men of Jabesh? Show how David appreciated it.

What resolve did he make when he became king?

How did Jerusalem become the Jewish capital?

What was "the Ark of the Lord"?

Quote a verse of the great processional hymn in bringing in the Ark.

LESSON VII

THE FALL OF DAVID

2 Samuel XI. and other parts as indicated.

Our study to-day is 2 Samuel *ch.* xi, and parts of the following chapters.

We have studied the various periods of David's life, and the Psalms commonly ascribed to each period. We have watched his youth in the quiet pasture fields where the influences of nature were deepening his thoughts of God. We have seen his friendship with Jonathan ennobling him still more. We have followed his years of adversity as an outlaw, bracing his moral nature, teaching himself restraint, and forcing him to cling more closely to God. Then in the last chapter we studied his early years of prosperity as a king, and they, too, also seemed to be deepening his religious life.

And now, at the age of fifty, totally against all reasonable expectations, we suddenly come upon the great catastrophe of his life.

§ 1. David's Sin

Whenever I hear of a really religious man (not a hypocrite) falling suddenly into a grave sin, my knowledge of life and character leads me to suspect at once that that fall was not so sudden as it seems. Something was wrong before. Some gradual neglect of prayer, some gradual yielding to some self-indulgence, some slacking of the moral tension of the man which outside people have not noticed. It is like as when a solid, firm-looking tree smashes off unexpectedly in a storm. When you examine it you find the dry rot beginning secretly at its centre.

I think David had been gradually yielding to self-indulgence and neglecting his duty. Don't you think the historian seems to suggest this? See *ch.* xi. *v.* 1—"It came to pass at the time when kings go forth to battle that David"—did what? Went out to battle? Ah, no. Nothing of the kind. He sent Joab and others on this errand of war; but he himself tarried behind in idle self-indulgence at Jerusalem. If he had been where his duty called him, out in the open field, if he had been sharing the hardy soldier's couch or the hard ground before the walls of Rabbah, the pages of the Bible might never have been sullied with this foul stain. Let us learn the lesson. The loosening of his moral tension; the lax walk; the self-indulgent living, were a preparation for his fall.

I cannot dwell on the wretched tale. How the king arose from his couch. How he looked down at evening from the roof, and beheld the beautiful young wife of one of his officers who was out with Joab before the walls of Rabbah. I have told you already of David's harem, and how new wives were added on, and of the whole degraded old-world life of kings with their wives. The coming of our Lord and His religion has made that impossible now. David's life was more like that of a Mohammedan sultan than that of a Christian king of our day. A Mohammedan sultan would not hesitate to add on any new wife whom he fancied, but I do not think that even a Mohammedan sultan would take the wife of one of his own brave officers. This David did. And he did it wickedly and treacherously.

He knew very well the shame of what he was doing. Then by-and-by he began to wish that her husband Uriah was dead. Did he murder him? Yes, I think I should call it distinctly murder. But I think David did not call it murder until after his repentance. When the devil tempts a man to a bad sin he generally makes it not look so bad at first. Murder Uriah! oh dear no; he would be quite shocked at that. This is what the devil whispered in his heart: "Send a message to Joab who is commanding the troops. In the first dangerous expedition let Uriah take the lead. Why should not Uriah go into danger as well as another? Some one must go. Why not Uriah?" But Uriah may escape after all. Ah! he may. Well, further precautions must be taken. Uriah must not come back alive to Jerusalem.

The king's word was law to Joab. Indeed, Joab had very good reason for wishing to have the king in his power. A forlorn hope was to be led next day, and Joab assigned to Uriah "the place where valiant men were," and the cruelly-wronged young soldier went bravely forth—to die. That evening a courier dashed up to the palace with Joab's despatch:—"The battle is over; the attack was repulsed, *and thy servant Uriah, the Hittite, is dead also.*" What a relief to David!

The villainous plot was successful. The faithful soldier had fallen in the path of duty, unconscious, let us hope, of his king's treachery, and when the decent mourning time was over the faithless Bathsheba became the wife of the king.

§ 2. David's Penitence

Does it seem to you impossible that David, or any man with the least bit of religion, could do such wickedness? Are you inclined to think David must have been a hypocrite with all his fine psalms and prayers? Yet even an earnest good man, if not watchful of his life, may, in an unguarded time, fall into a very hateful sin. When he does, the only sign that he has not forsaken God is the depth and bitterness of his repentance. So you have to judge whether David's penitence was very deep and bitter.

You must remember that in those dark ages of the world before our Lord came, men would not think so badly of these sins as Christian people do. I have been teaching you that all through these lessons. The coming of Christ made an immense difference. The human race was in its spiritual childhood before. The race came of age, as it were, when He came. He was the light of the world, and conscience sprang into fuller power and clearer insight when God became incarnate and the full gift of the Holy Spirit was given to Christians.

David lived in a dark age. Probably other kings of his time would not have troubled very much about this sin. You must compare David not with some saintly Christian king, but with the Sultan of Turkey or an Arab chief at Bagdad. And then you will see how deep was the penitence of David, and how miserable he was at having grieved his God. You will see that one of the most wonderful things in all literature is the 51st Psalm, the expression, it is said, of David's penitence when condemned for his sin. You remember how Nathan the prophet came to condemn him. Repeat for me Nathan's parable "The Ewe Lamb" (chap. xii). What did it mean? Yes. That David who had so many wives and friends cruelly took away the wife of his young captain. And when the prophet brought it all home to him, hear how he feels. Listen to his heartfelt cry as he bows before the prophet. "Oh, I have sinned, I have sinned against the Lord." Listen to that touching confession in the 51st Psalm, which the title ascribes to the time of this visit of Nathan:—

> "Have mercy on me, O God after Thy great loving kindness;
> According to the multitude of Thy tender mercies,
>   Blot out my transgressions.
> Wash me thoroughly from my wickedness,
> And cleanse me from my sin."

Read it all over with wonder at such penitence in that age of the world, before Homer had sung about the Siege of Troy, before Romulus and Remus were suckled by the wolf. Notice that he makes out no case for himself. He pleads no extenuating circumstances. He says no word about begging to be let off his punishment, which is often our chief thought in our penitential prayers.

This is the penitential prayer of a man who knows he is going to be punished, and is content to be punished, provided that at any cost God would make him a clean heart and renew a right spirit within him. Surely it must be because of his faith in God, because he knew that the Father punishes for His child's good, and will not hold back the rod for any crying of the child.

I think he was restless and miserable even before Nathan came. Many writers think that the 32nd Psalm is his and refers to his remembrance of that whole wretched time before he confessed his sin.

> "Blessed is the man whose transgression is forgiven, whose sin is covered.

> *   *   *   *   *   *   *   *

> When I kept silence my bones waxed old through my daily complaining:
> For day and night Thy hand was heavy upon me,
> My moisture was changed as with the drought of summer.
> I acknowledged my sin unto Thee, and mine iniquity have I not hid.
> I said I will confess my transgressions unto the Lord,
> And Thou forgavest the iniquity of my sin."

That was how the stern love of God tortured him, and then the visit of Nathan and the parable of the ewe lamb brought things to a crisis. It is an awful thing to think that he could have so deeply sinned. Yet it is some comfort that he should have so deeply repented.

§ 3. David's Punishment

Some people mockingly say, "Ah! how nicely and easily David got off." "I have sinned against the Lord!" he cries to the prophet. And the prophet says, "The Lord also hath put away thy sin!!" It seems very easy and pleasant, people say, that men can go and sow their wild oats, and then get off scot free without being properly punished. That David, who was guilty of this dastardly crime, should be as well off as his neighbours, who had had a similar temptation and resisted it.

Never you believe that. No man ever got off scot free from his sins. God's forgiveness does not remove all the consequences of sin. It is true that God will receive you from wider condemnation. God will forgive you. God will strengthen you for a holier life. God will rejoice as a father over his child who has come back. It is true, too, that some great souls, through the depth and agony of penitence, may win back even more than they have lost by their sin. But do not you ever believe that God's forgiveness will abolish the results of your sin. That sin, though forgiven, will leave, perhaps, in your life—in your characters—in your weakness—often in your position and reputation—its traces and consequences, that may cling to you while life remains.

It is necessary to say this strongly, for it seems to me the danger of our day is that we are so anxious to tell men of the goodness of God that the righteousness of God is almost forgotten and that sin does not seem a very terrible thing at all.

Young men sometimes talk lightly of sowing their wild oats. They forget that wild oats have a trick of growing where we don't expect them; that there are consequences which God will not take away; that the great law is true, even for him who is forgiven, "Whatsoever a man soweth, that shall he reap."

David let off lightly, they say! Was he, though? Look at his after life. He prayed that God would forgive him; that God would purify him. And God answered him. And God will answer you, too, if you ask Him to forgive you; if you ask Him to purify you—even after you have sown your wild oats. But before you do it, better see how God answered David.

(1) First came the death of the child. For days and nights the father watched and prayed in misery over the dying sufferings of his little child. He felt that it was all a punishment for his sin.

(2) Then he had all his life Joab bullying him. Joab who knew his guilty secret about Uriah's death.

(3) Then came the discovery of hateful abominable sins in his own family—the children sinning in the steps of their father. Oh what a fearful punishment was that which David had brought upon himself.

(4) And then came the blow that almost broke his heart—the treachery and revolt of his beloved Absalom, the corpse of his boy hanging in the wood of

Ephraim, slain in rebellion against his father and his king (chap. xviii.).

David let off lightly! was he? Think of that trembling old man in the chamber over the gate waiting to hear the result of the battle. See the agonized wringing of his hands. Hear that cry from the depths of his tortured soul eight times repeated—"Oh, Absalom, my son, my son, would God I had died for thee, Absalom, Absalom, Absalom, my son, my son."

That picture of the chamber over the gate belongs to all time—to our day as well as David's—the agonized father sorrowing over his boy gone wrong. How many such do I know to-day!

> Somewhere at every hour,
> The watchman on the tower,
> Sees messengers that bear
> The tidings of despair.
>   O Absalom, my son!
>
> The boy goes forth from the door,
> Who shall return no more,
> With him their joy departs,
> The light goes out in their hearts.
>
> In the chamber over the gate
> They sit disconsolate,
> And for ever the cry will be
> Would God I had died for thee.
>   O Absalom, my son!

§ 4. David's Hope

Will any one dare say now that David was let off lightly?

And I have not said the worst yet. David's own character suffered fearfully for his sin. I don't want to discourage any penitent. There are cases where men in their deep sorrow for sin have grown to be even stronger and more religious after it. But they are not many.

David's was a spoiled life from that day forward. Henceforth, we hear no more of noble heroic deeds—no more joyous activity—no more glad consciousness of his people's love. The narrative is singularly silent about him. He seems to have been in broken health. He originates nothing. He does nothing. It is a disappointing close to a once noble life.

Yet there is something else to be said. The lines of my picture are too crude and harsh to portray aright the end of David's life. True, it was a sad end. True, the consequences of his sin darkened it. Yet there must have been a peace and comfort amid it all in the thought that the father had forgiven him, and had a good purpose in his suffering. I once saw a mother punish her boy by ordering him to bed for the day without picture books or games. He went sullenly enough. By-and-by, as she passed, he called her in to forgive him, and to tell her how sorry he was. And in a moment her arms were around him, and he was kissed and forgiven. But his penalty remained. He had still to stay his full time in bed. Yes; but it was all so different now that mother had forgiven him and made friends with him, and he knew that it was her wise love that refused to set him free.

I think it was like that with David, and I think it was because it was like that—because he was a sinning, suffering man, trusting in God, resting in God, struggling nearer to God in spite of his pain—that his Psalms are such a help to poor, sinning, suffering, struggling men to-day.

And so we finish the story of David's life, beautiful and hopeful at the beginning, saddening and disappointing at the end. And yet hopeful there, too, as we think of its new beginning in the new strange life within the veil. Maybe his old friend Jonathan was there to meet him, he who once "strengthened David's hands in God." Ah, God is very good to His poor children. Every man who spoils his life here must for ever suffer loss in some degree for it. But God will do the best possible even for him. To the Lord our God belong mercies and forgivenesses though we have rebelled against Him.

QUESTIONS FOR LESSON VII

What was the great sin of David's life?

When a good man falls into a great sin is the fall usually sudden or by degrees?

What is the warning here for us?

Who was Uriah the Hittite?

Show how sorry David was for this sin.

Did God forgive him?

But did God punish him too? How?

How could there be punishment with forgiveness? Illustrate from my story of the little boy in bed.

LESSON VIII

SOLOMON

The passages in 1 Kings here referred to.

§ 1. Religious Education

Next comes King Solomon, the son of David and Bathsheba. (Notice that we have now come to the FIRST BOOK OF KINGS.) I wonder what sort of childhood Solomon had? We know little of it, but I think it must have been sad and unsatisfactory. The boy was born in a dark, troubled time. The sins of his father were bringing their retribution. The people were suspicious. The king was growing old, and gloomy, and fretful. The members of his family were not behaving well. The little boy would probably be with his mother in the harem, and I don't think Bathsheba would be a mother to influence him for good. And I am quite sure that degrading palace life in the women's quarters would not be good for him. All these jealous women, each plotting for the king's favour for her own children, each trying in any silly way to pass the weary, monotonous day. We get glimpses of such life from the Indian zenana missionaries to-day.

Then as he grew up he would be in the midst of the palace scheming and crimes, when Absalom killed his brother and fled, and, later, when Absalom rose in rebellion, and King David had to fly from Jerusalem, taking Bathsheba and Solomon with him. Would the boy ever forget that miserable time, and the sobbing of the old king when Absalom lay dead in the wood of Ephraim?

It is hard to understand how he grew up to be religious at all. There must have been some influence. Somebody must have taught him high thoughts of good. Perhaps his father helped him. Perhaps 2 Samuel xii. 25 is intended to tell us that Nathan, the prophet, had the boy in charge.

§ 2. Solomon's Youth

I shall but touch his life at three points. Solomon's youth; Solomon in all his glory; Solomon's old age.

While he was still a lad, came the coronation day, when, amid the shouts of the rejoicing people, "Zadok, the priest, and Nathan, the prophet, anointed Solomon king." He was still only a lad. Hopefully, earnestly, he began his reign. As Saul did. As David did. In Gibeon (1 Kings iii. 5, etc.) he heard in a vision God calling him, "Choose what I shall give thee," and nobly he replied, "Lord, I am but as a little child. Give me a wise and understanding heart that I may judge this great people." And the saying pleased the Lord, and He said, "Because thou hast not asked for thyself long life or riches, nor the life of thine enemies, lo! I have given thee a wise and understanding heart, and I have given thee besides that which thou hast not asked for, riches and honour," etc. So Solomon "was wiser than all men." He spake 3,000 proverbs, and his songs were 1,005 (*ch.* iv. 32). And still while he was young there was given to him the glorious task of building the temple of God.

Surely he got a good start in life. Is it not very touching to see all the good starts in life which end in disappointment? It seems as if God were eternally hopeful about His children. He gave Saul a grand start in life, and Saul disappointed Him. He gave David a grand start, and David disappointed Him. And now He gives young Solomon a similar grand start, and He is going to be disappointed again. It is touching, but it is beautiful. It is the Father's way all through. See the crowd of little children brought to Baptism to be regenerated with the gift of His Holy Spirit, and how they disappoint Him. And yet He goes on blessing the young lives as they come. Those who don't get a good start here are bound, we believe, to get it somewhere. And He is watching them all. For ever there must be joy in His heart over one that repenteth. For ever there must be pain over one who fails to come back. What a shame to disappoint Him!

§ 3. "Solomon in All His Glory"

Twenty years have passed when we contemplate Solomon again.

Solomon in all his glory. Listen:—

"And Solomon reigned over all the kingdoms from the river unto the land of the Philistines and to the border of Egypt . . . And these were the princes that Solomon had . . . And Solomon's provision for one day was thirty measures of fine flour, and sixty measures of meal, ten fat oxen, twenty pasture oxen, one hundred sheep, besides harts, roebucks, fallow-deer and fatted fowl."

"And all King Solomon's drinking vessels were of gold, and all the vessels of the house of the forest of Lebanon were of fine gold; none were of silver; it was nothing accounted of in the days of Solomon. For the king had at sea a navy of Tharshish to bring gold and silver, and ivory and apes and peacocks. So King Solomon exceeded all the kings of the earth for riches and for wisdom." (See parts of *ch.* iv. and *ch.* x.)

Does it not almost startle you with a sense of gorgeousness, and prosperity, and wealth, and barbaric splendour, and crowds of kings and princes, and peoples wondering and applauding? Such a court, such peace, and prosperity, and prosperous trading. No wonder people talked about the glory of Solomon. No wonder that our Lord should make the comparison, "Even Solomon in all his glory," etc.

Yet somehow in all the glory you get a sense of

94

something secular and worldly, a feeling as if all the profusion of gold, and silver, and ivory, and apes, and peacocks, and all the rest were closing in the scene and shutting out the view of God, and Duty, and the Invisible World. One beautiful scene there is in *ch.* viii., before the worldly glory had eaten the heart out of his religion. It was when the temple was finished and Solomon uttered that exquisitely beautiful consecration prayer, "Hear thou in heaven, thy dwelling-place, and when thou hearest, forgive!" (Read part of this prayer in *ch.* viii.) This teaches us that there was much good in Solomon as well as evil. I think the evil was beginning even then. Turn to *ch.* ix., a vision of God again like that vision in his youthful days in Gibeon long ago. And yet unlike it. Notice the tone of warning about it. The Lord accepts his gift of the temple and hallows it, and then come the words to Solomon himself (*v.* 4), "If thou wilt walk before me as David thy father walked in integrity of heart and uprightness . . . then will I establish thy throne, etc. . . . But if ye shall at all turn from following me, then I will cast out Israel, and this house will I cast out . . . because they have taken hold of other gods and served them." It makes one think that evil must have been beginning in Solomon's life even then that he needed this warning against the "other gods."

§ 4. Solomon's Old Age

Now we come to the third period. (Read *ch.* xi. 1-4.) The Bible passes over the intermediate years, the intermediate steps of his soul's career. Straight and sudden it plunges into "It came to pass when Solomon was old that his wives turned away his heart from God." One wonders how this should happen to a religious man, only we know that sort of thing does not happen all at once. His heart must have long been moving away from God before he could join in the filthy impurities of the idol worship and turn apostate to his God and his national religion.

One can easily guess how it happened. In the days of his glory we read of his great commercial speculations. He sent ships trading to foreign lands. He sailed himself to Ezion Geber to see the place. He had all his great undertakings to look after, his towns and his forts, and the coming home of his merchant ships, and his great building schemes, and his countless officers, etc. He had a delightfully busy, exciting life, and sometimes a man may get so wrapped up in that as to hurry his prayers and forget his God. And then, too, this would bring him into intercourse with other peoples and kings richer, and grander, and more accomplished than the quiet Israelites. It was easy to forget that they were heathen, godless men and women.

You can understand Solomon was very like ourselves. The same may happen to any young man to-day. He has been brought up in a godly home and learned to love God. He goes out into the world, to business, to college. He meets gay, godless, attractive men, handsome, pleasant, accomplished women. They have very pleasant manners and many things to attract him. It is easy to forget that they are worldly and irreligious, seldom go to church, don't care about the unselfish service to which Christ calls us all. I think Solomon began like that. Then he began to admire some of the beautiful heathen princesses till the court of Jerusalem was filled with women of the Amorites, Moabites, Hittites, Zidonians. They brought their priests and their idols until the city which David dedicated by bringing the Ark of God became almost a heathen city. And Solomon, to please them, joined in idol worship, and the people saw their king an apostate from God. It was very horrible. It was even worse than merely forsaking God. Indian missionaries have told me of such horrible, filthy rites connected with idol worship that it would be impossible to tell you of them.

§ 5. *The Sternness of God's Love*

It is a miserable story, but so terribly natural and easy to believe from our own knowledge of life to-day. Poor Solomon in all his glory! Do you think he was happy when he was old? Ah! thank God, no! Whatever happiness he may get while he is young, no irreligious man is happy when he is old. And if he has once been religious he is more miserable still. You may be quite sure this poor old king was not happy with all his grandeur.

It is a poor, desolate, withered old head, old and grey before its time, that is represented[1] in the Book of Ecclesiastes as telling his views of life. Listen to the king who had accomplished so much: "I looked on all

[1]Whoever wrote the book of Ecclesiastes it is intended to present Solomon's point of view.

that my hands had wrought, and on the labour that I had laboured to do; and, behold, all is vanity and vexation of spirit, and there is no profit under the sun." (Ecclesiastes ii. 1). Listen to the wise man, famed for his wisdom: "In much wisdom there is much grief. He that increaseth knowledge increaseth sorrow. Therefore, I hated life because all is vanity."

Don't be sorry that he was miserable. Be glad that God did not leave him to himself. That is the way in which the strong, stern love of the father tries to get back His child. That is why the prodigal in the far country feels the mighty famine in that land. That is why every worldly heart in its old age to-day is without real happiness. It is the rod of the Good Shepherd seeking His sheep, "if so be that He may find it."

Did God find Solomon? The Bible is silent. The Early Church was doubtful. There is a great picture in Florence of Solomon rising from the dead and looking right and left as if not knowing what was his place. But I like to think of that prophecy of his childhood, "I will be his father, and he shall be My son. If he commit iniquity, I will chasten him; but My mercy shall not depart from him." I like to think of that sorrowful old age. I like to think of that which is true for ever. "To the Lord our God belong mercies and forgivenesses, though we have rebelled against Him."

§ 6. Solomon's End

And so at last Solomon died. We know not how. The Bible does not tell us. But the Koran, the Mohammedan

Bible, has a legend of his death which seems almost a parable. It tells how the old king entered the temple robed and crowned, and stood between the pillars leaning on his ebony staff. And as he stood there silent, facing the altar, God's hand touched him, and he died as he stood. But because of his sacred staff and ring, none dared approach him. And so he stood there many days like a painted king, with the death stare in his eyes. And the priests and the worshippers gazed at him there, dead and magnificent. And still he stood—until a worm within the magic staff had gnawed it through, and flat on his face the dead king fell, and out of the dust they picked his golden crown.

Is it not a parable of his fall—the worm gnawing in the centre of his staff—the dry rot setting in in the centre of his life? "I the Preacher was king over Israel in Jerusalem. Vanity of vanities, saith the Preacher; all is vanity." (Ecclesiastes i. 2).

What was this worm at the centre of the staff—this dry rot setting in in the centre of the life? Worldliness. The world means life lived apart from God. What was Solomon's world? The gold and silver—the pomp and power—the splendid commerce—the attractive strangers—the learned Egypt—the busy Sidon—the princesses of Moab and Ammon and Heth. The world without God.

What is your world? Whatever attracts you in a similar way—if it also be without God. What harm, young people ask, in this dashing, lively, fascinating world, with its keen interests, its exciting pleasures?

What harm? Just that it is without God—that it is low, that it is earthy, that it sees and lives for only the visible—for the houses, and servants, and carriages, and pleasures, and money, and the praise of men. It never looks up to the invisible world of God, and Right, and Duty, and Heaven, and the Holy Angels.

That was the dry rot in Solomon's staff. That is the lesson of Solomon's life. "My little children, love not the world, neither the things that are in the world. If any man love the world, the love of the Father is not in him." (John ii. 15).

(Read the passages in 1 Kings referred to above.)

QUESTIONS FOR LESSON VIII

Tell me something of Solomon's greatness.

Was Solomon a good man like David?

Mothers have much to do with this. Who was Solomon's mother? Was she good?

Tell me of Solomon's choice in his dream. Did he live up to that?

Who "turned away Solomon's heart from God"?

Tell the curious Arab story of Solomon's death and the lesson from it.

LESSON IX

REHOBOAM AND JEROBOAM

1 Kings XII.

Now we come to the division of the kingdom. The nation had grown so idolatrous and so filthy in its heathen worship that the Holy God could no longer allow it to keep its position. All through history God's punishments keep falling on nations like this. And the punishments are worked out by people who do not know that they are working out God's punishments. The nation was to be broken into two parts as God's judgment on its sin.[1] Alas! it never was reunited again. For 300 years the northern kingdom of Israel, the larger portion, existed with varying fortunes until at length the King of Assyria carried its people captive to Babylon. For 100 years longer the smaller kingdom of Judah survived, until Nebuchadnezzar swept it away into the Babylonian captivity. I shall not trouble you much with historical or political details. Remember these broad facts—the division of the kingdom—the existence of Israel for 300 years and of Judah for 400 years until

[1] 1 Kings xii. 13-24.

101

each was overthrown and carried off to exile. Instead of going into the details of kings, and battles, and politics, etc., I shall seek out the most important events and the lessons which they teach as we go down this 400 years of history.

§ 1. Coronation Day

Solomon is dead, and his son Rehoboam is called to the throne. He, too, is young, and, as far as we can judge, has been badly brought up. We have already seen the faults of Solomon's training. His mother, Bathsheba, and his life in the harem would probably have evil influence on his childhood.

But Rehoboam's case is much worse. Solomon's mother, at least, was a Jewess, and brought up in the Jewish religion. Rehoboam's mother was who? (1 Kings xiv. 31), Yes, Naamah, an Ammonitess. She was evidently one of these idolatrous foreign princesses who had been trained in the horrible worship of Moloch. A mother has a powerful influence in this matter. But just think, if your mother worshipped a horrible idol to whom little children were sacrificed? And if she took you to worship with her. That would be your notion of God. So you see when judging some of these ancient kings we must be very gentle and make all allowances. They had not good training in childhood.

I suppose Rehoboam grew up as an idle young prince, with many young nobles to be his comrades and to flatter him. Just the way to make him vain, and proud, and conceited. Now came the coronation day.

You remember the coronation of Saul, and David, and Solomon? So all the people assembled at Shechem to make Rehoboam king. But they were not quite so eager and unanimous as in former coronations. Perhaps they were doubtful about the young king. Certainly they were dissatisfied at all the burdens Solomon had put on them. All his greatness and grandeur had to be kept up by forced taxes and forced labour of the people. I don't think they had been very happy under Solomon. So now, before crowning the new king, they want to ask him some questions.

There is another young man mentioned here who seems to be the leader and speaker for the people (*vv.* 2, 3). What do we know previously about Jeroboam? (*ch.* xi. 26-41). Yes. He was evidently an able, powerful man, and had already got into trouble with Solomon (*ch.* xi.). Yes, why? He was an officer in Solomon's works, and the prophet Ahijah told him that God would punish Solomon and the nation for their idolatry and wickedness by this rending of the nation, and that he, Jeroboam, was to be king of the ten tribes. I suppose he was indiscreet enough to talk about this until Solomon heard it, and Jeroboam had to flee for his life to Egypt (*ch.* xi. 40). There he grew into favour with the king of Egypt, and married an Egyptian princess.

§ 2. *Young Men's Advice*

Now he is back and mingling with the people, and hearing their complaints and sympathizing with them, and it would seem as if he were their speaker before the king. What did the people demand? (xii. 4). Yes. A very fair claim it would seem, "Don't crush us down with enforced taxes and enforced labour, as your father did, and we will serve you."

What a fool he was not to declare himself at once their friend and protector. What does he do? Promises to consider. Then he seeks the wise old men who knew his father, and wisely they counselled him—what? (*v.* 7). "Serve them and speak kind words to them." Ah! that was good advice if he would take it. But he would not. He called his young comrades, proud, pert, foolish, young fellows like himself. What do they advise? (*vv.* 10, 11). So silly. No respect for the people. No effort to understand the feelings of the oppressed. "Show them that you are a king. How dare they speak thus to you? Treat them like dogs. Tell them you will be a great deal more to be feared than your father." And the silly young fool of a king thinks it sounds quite grand to tell his people, "My little finger shall be thicker than my father's loins."

To feel with and for others, and to "put ourselves in their place," to treat them with respect, would make the world a great deal a happier place.

§ 3. *To Your Tents, O Israel!*

I daresay Jeroboam was not sorry to see this foolish impertinence. The people listened to the words of Rehoboam. For a moment there was a pause and then a fierce stirring anger, and then there rang out over the plains of Shechem the rebellious shout that must have frightened the young king, "To your tents, O Israel!"

And before he could say or do anything to prevent it three-fourths of the great assembly were marching to their tents in open rebellion. Nevermore would they serve under the house of David! I think the king was sorry then (*ch.* xii. 18). He sent a messenger to them perhaps to make friends—perhaps, indeed, only to collect the taxes. But the angry men of Israel stoned him with stones, and after that it was too late for any hope of reconciliation.

So only the men of Judah obeyed Rehoboam. The ten tribes of Israel chose Jeroboam, the son of Nebat, and the nation was broken into separate parts. God's punishment had fallen. I don't think Jeroboam cared about God's will any more than Rehoboam. He only wanted to satisfy his own ambition. But that is the wonderful thing in God's ruling the world. Even men's ambition, and anger, and wickedness are made to carry out God's will without the men themselves ever thinking of it. Rehoboam's pride and folly, Jeroboam's ambitious scheming, in the end worked out God's will. What do you think was the great instance of this in the world's history? Surely the spite and bigotry of the Jews crucifying our Lord on Calvary.

§ 4. Jeroboam's Calves

Now, what was God's promise to Jeroboam when He gave him the ten tribes? "If thou wilt hearken unto all that I command thee, and will walk in my ways, and do what is right," (*ch.* xi. 38). You see, with God it is always the question of right and wrong. That is the supreme thing in God's sight. Whatever way things go, it is the law of God for ever and ever, that the best thing in the whole world is to do the right, and the worst thing in the whole world is to do the wrong. Whatever the consequences may *seem* to be at the moment, this is the law of God for ever and ever.

Did Jeroboam do what God wished? (*ch.* xii. 26, etc.). You see he would not trust God. God said, "If you do the right I will bless you in your new kingdom." But Jeroboam, like so many others who think themselves very clever, was stupid enough to forget the great law of God about right and wrong. They think "I will do a clever thing, even if it be not quite right, and so I will make myself secure." So with men and women, and boys and girls, who think by a clever act of dishonesty or untruthfulness to advance themselves. It is an awfully stupid thing to think yourself and wrong-doing more powerful to help you than God and right-doing would be. Mind you don't be such a fool as Jeroboam.

You understand what his cleverness aimed at? If all the people went to the temple at Jerusalem to worship they might, he thought, at length wish to join again with Rehoboam in his capital at Jerusalem, and so might cast out Jeroboam (*ch.* xiii. 27). So what did he do? Yes. Made golden calves as images of God, and set them up for worship in his own part of the kingdom. Do you remember a similar case before (Exodus xxxii. 4), when Aaron made the golden calf? You see Jeroboam, like Aaron, had lived in Egypt where the golden bull and golden calf were to the Egyptians the signs of their God. That was what put the thought into the minds

106

of both. I don't think they or the people were stupid enough to think that a dead calf of gold was God. But it was something to remind them of God. They thought it would be easier to worship the invisible God if they had something before them to look at. God had warned them in the second commandment not to do this. To set up bestial creatures as reminders of the Holy God would soon make the men and women bestial themselves. For horrible wickedness used to follow such worship. It is too ugly to speak of. And Jeroboam worked all that evil to the people's souls in order to keep his kingdom safe.

For a while his plan succeeded. But soon trouble after trouble came. A prophet of God came and cursed his altar, and it broke into pieces at his word (*ch.* xiii). Then (*ch.* xvi.) comes the touching, sorrowful story of the king's little boy falling sick, and all the grandeur and success could not make up for that little boy's pain. So the king sent his wife, that Egyptian princess, and she went away into the mountains to find the old prophet Ahijah, who had long ago prophesied that Jeroboam should be king. She disguised herself like a poor woman, and she thought that as the old prophet was so blind he would not know her to be the queen. But his quick ear recognized her walk, and he sternly pronounced on her the punishment of God. "Because your husband King Jeroboam has done evil above all that were before him, go back to your house, and when your feet enter into the city, the child shall die. And all Israel shall mourn for him, for he is the only one of the house of Jeroboam who has in him any good thing towards the

Lord." So when the poor, frightened mother stepped over the threshold, she heard the crying of her maids. The boy was dead. God had taken him away from the wicked home into the beautiful Paradise land, and the king, with all his success and all his grandeur, had to look upon his dead child and learn that it was his own wickedness had lost him his boy.

Ah! this success and grandeur were not much comfort to him that night, you may be sure, as he heard the poor mother crying over her dead. I think that night Jeroboam wished he had been a good man, and done the right, and trusted God.

(Read 1 Kings xii.)

QUESTIONS FOR LESSON IX

How did the Israelite Kingdom get broken into two? Names of the two?

Who were Rehoboam and Jeroboam?

Tell of Rehoboam's foolishness.

Why did Jeroboam set up the golden calves?

Who else in earlier days set up a golden calf for worship?

Which of the Ten Commandments forbids worshipping God through images?

AHAB AND ELIJAH, PART I

1 Kings XV. 29 to end of XVII.

It must be kept clearly in mind that after the Division of the nation there is a history of Israel, the Northern Kingdom, lasting 300 years, until it was carried away into Assyria, and a history of Judah, the Southern Kingdom, lasting 400 years, until the exile to Babylon. These histories are interwoven in the Bible, but for clearness we keep them distinct. We continue now the story of Israel, the Northern Kingdom.

After the death of Jeroboam comes a list of unimportant kings and of ugly crimes ending with the murder of the drunken King Elah, by Zimri, one of the captains of the host. This led to a revolution and to the rise of the house of Omri. Omri was a strong, brave, wicked king (1 Kings xvi. 25). At his death he was succeeded by his son Ahab. And the story of King Ahab and Elijah which we are now to tell is one of the best known in the whole history of Israel.

§ 1. King Ahab

When King Omri died he left to his son Ahab a prosperous kingdom. And the young king was evidently a clever and ambitious man, likely to increase the prosperity still farther. The history speaks of "the cities which he built, and his ivory house, and his might, and the wars which he warred," suggesting at least that he was a man of considerable ability. Perhaps for that reason he was the more attracted to friendship with the kings around him.

Since Solomon's time there had been a good deal of intercourse between Israel and the surrounding nations. Many of them were much grander and richer and were powerful and more polished than the simple nation of Israel. But, unfortunately, grandeur, riches and power and polish were the chief things they aimed at. What was the chief thing that God was teaching Israel to aim at? Yes. Righteousness. To try to be righteous, just, holy, pure—that was to be the supreme aim of the nation. That was why God sent His prophets to teach them. That was why God sent His sharp punishments to discipline them. Israel was chosen, not for its own sake, but for the sake of all humanity, to teach the world righteousness. So the Bible for all the world has come to us from Israel. You see at once the great difference between Israel and other nations. The aim of Israel was? Righteousness. The aim of the others? Power, greatness, pleasure, etc. And I think this will show you that there might be danger in Israel mixing too much with these other nations with the lower aims.

§ 2. Jezebel

One of these nations was that of Tyre and Sidon (show the places on the map), ruled at that time by Ethbaal, lord of Phœnicia. He had made himself king by murdering his brother, and he was not only king, but also high priest of Ashtoreth, the filthy goddess of the Sidonians. So you see he was not a very satisfactory friend for any king of Israel.

Ahab visited at his court, and I suppose was attracted by the beauty of his daughter Isabel, or Jezebel, as her name is in the Bible. By-and-by they were married, and the young king took home his bride to his own land. And I dare say there were great rejoicings and festivities to welcome the bride to Israel. Ah! little they knew what a curse she was to bring them. For, first, she was as wicked as her father, King Ethbaal, and, second, she was a most determined worshipper of the filthy gods of Phœnicia. Baal was the god of Power, Ashtoreth was the goddess whose worship was carried on with such vile sins as cannot be mentioned. Think what that meant in the nation of the God of Righteousness and Purity and Holiness. It was much worse than the worship of Jeroboam's golden calves. Bad as they were, he at least meant to represent Jehovah, "who brought you up out of the land of Egypt." (1 Kings xii. 28). It was very wrong to represent Jehovah by golden calves. But the worship of Baal and Ashtoreth was the casting out of God's worship altogether, and the bringing the gods of power and of impurity into the place of the God of Righteousness.

§ 3. The Persecution

In a few years a great stately temple of Baal was set up in Samaria and hundreds of idolatrous priests and prophets came to the court of Jezebel. She went, of course, with all her court to worship the idol. And when queens do this it soon becomes fashionable. The Israelite ladies soon followed the example of the Tyrians. By-and-by many of the men followed. Then some of the priests and prophets of Jehovah were drawn into the new worship, until at last it became a great national apostasy.

Ahab, I think, was weak rather than wicked. His wife was a much stronger character than he, and so he was soon an apostate from God, a worshipper of the horrible Sidonian gods. Then arose THE PERSECUTION OF THE PROPHETS. Queen Jezebel seemed determined not only to bring in the worship of Baal, but to cast out the worship of God. A fierce persecution of the prophets of God was begun. They were hunted through the land and murdered where they were found. Some of them fled. Some of them hid in caves in the mountains of Samaria. One good man, an officer of the court named Obadiah, hid a hundred of them by fifties in a cave and fed them secretly every day with bread and water. For years the cruel persecution went on, until it seemed that no prophet of God remained in the land.

§ 4. Elijah

Then at last God, who had been watching over all, interfered. And then came Elijah. It is a wonderful story.

112

We know nothing about Elijah before this except that he belonged to the wild mountains of Gilead. His boyhood, his youth, his training, his communion with God in the mountains, all about him up to this is absolutely unknown. Suddenly, in the face of Ahab's power, in the face of Jezebel's cruelty, in the face of the people's apostasy from their ancient faith, a solitary man, a wild prophet from the wilderness, comes out into the polished wicked city of Samaria to fight alone for God and the Right. To fight *alone*. That is what makes Elijah so grand.

He knew that his life was in his hand. Jezebel's prophet-hunters had been for months upon his trail. And yet he walks boldly into the city of Ahab and startles the king one day in the midst of his court. "Elijah the Tishbite said unto Ahab, As the Lord God of Israel liveth before whom I stand there shall not be dew nor rain these years but according to my word." And then suddenly as he came he disappeared; but he left a great dread behind him in Samaria. Any threat about stopping of dew and rain in a hot Eastern summer would greatly frighten people. If the dew and rain stopped, then would come famine and misery, the cattle dropping dead in the withered pastures, the people dropping dead of hunger and thirst in the streets. No more terrible thing could happen to hot Eastern lands than a continued drought.

You can imagine the anger of Ahab and Jezebel and the court of Samaria. Somehow conscience would frighten them into feeling that they deserved punishment. Somehow they could not get over the fear that that stern prophet of righteousness had something to do with God and might have the power given him by God to hold back the rain from them. Over every part of the country they sought for him most closely. They made each town and village declare with a solemn oath whether they knew his whereabouts. If they could only catch him they felt something might be done.

How did Elijah get power to send rain? Read James v. 17. He prayed earnestly that it should not rain, as God's threatened punishment for idolatry (Deuteronomy xi. 17). And God had answered his prayer. And he believed that God would answer it.

Meantime the blazing sun poured down upon the pastures, and the rivers ran low and the streams dried up and the cattle were gasping with thirst. In the early morning the farmer came and put his hand on the grass and found no dew or moisture. Months and months passed. How they longed for rain! How they watched that hot clear sky all day for any trace of a cloud! I dare say they had prayers for rain in the idol's temple and asked the ugly big idol to save them in their trouble. I dare say, too, that some of them began to feel sorry that they had given up the God who had so blessed their nation before.

§ 5. The Widow of Zarephath

Oh, if they could only find Elijah! Perhaps they could coax him or bribe him or frighten him. Perhaps he would feel pitiful and pray for them to God. But he had vanished out of their sight. They never thought of searching for him near Jezebel's old home in Sidon.

By the guidance of God he had wandered about till he came to the village of Zarephath in Jezebel's land, where he was told the Lord would provide a widow woman to sustain him. The drought had spread to Zarephath too. And as the prophet came to the gate he found a poor widow gathering sticks. These things seem chance, but Elijah knew that God had to do with it. She and her child were starving in the famine. But in her sore trouble she could think of his trouble too. He was fainting with thirst.

"Will you bring me a little water?" he asked.

Yes, she would.

"And a little morsel of bread."

"I would if I could, but as the Lord thy God liveth I have only just enough to give my son and myself one last morsel before we die." I dare say Elijah guessed that she would not have eaten much herself of that last morsel. No mother would. Then with that deep confidence in his God the prophet declared to her, "Thy barrel of meal shall not waste, neither thy cruse of oil fail, until the day that the Lord sendeth rain." And that poor widow of Sidon trusted him and prepared the food, and for months and months she took meal out of that barrel and oil out of that cruse and they never seemed to grow less. And Elijah lived on there with her and her boy, and I am sure she learned much about God and about righteousness.

Then one day came her great sorrow; the boy was dying. The boy was dead. And the poor creature thought of the holiness of the man of God, and she thought of a great sin away back in her past life, and she put the two thoughts together. "My son is dead in punishment for my sin." Then she turned fiercely on Elijah. But the heart of that stern prophet was very soft and pitiful to her in her sorrow. He took up the little dead boy into his chamber and he prayed and prayed, oh, so earnestly. "O Lord my God, I pray Thee let this child's soul come into him again!" Do you think that God ought always to answer these terrible cries of longing for a dead child? I think He might, only that it would be such a loss to the child to come back. I wonder how long Elijah waited. I wonder how long the mother waited below, frightened and excited and afraid to hope. Can't you imagine the scene when by-and-by he came down those stairs and put the little child into her arms alive! One of the early writers of the Church, St. Jerome, tells of an old tradition that this boy followed and served Elijah and became afterwards the famous prophet Jonah. It is nice to see this gentle, loving side of the stern Elijah. Oh, he had soon to show a very different side. That will be in the next chapter.

Don't you like to think of our Lord being taught as a child this story that I am now teaching you? Do you remember how he spoke of Elijah and the widow of Sarepta? (St. Luke iv. 26).

(Read 1 Kings xvi. 29 to end, and ch. xvii.)

116

QUESTIONS FOR LESSON X

Which of the two kingdoms are we now reading about—Israel or Judah?

Who were: (1) Ahab, (2) Jezebel, (3) Elijah, (4) Obadiah?

What was the worship and what was the character of Jezebel's country?

What did she do to destroy the worship of God in Israel?

What punishment did Elijah threaten?

Tell of the suffering it brought.

Tell the story of Elijah and the widow's son.

AHAB AND ELIJAH, PART II

1 Kings XVIII.

Three years Elijah had been in hiding. Three years the drought had been on Israel. Then the word of the Lord came to Elijah, "Go show thyself unto Ahab. I will send rain upon the earth."

§ 1. Elijah's Challenge

The land was now in a terrible state. The pastures were withered brown under the sun, the river beds were dry. The cattle were dying in the fields. The people were sinking into hopeless despair. Ahab was at his wits' end. Oh! if he could catch Elijah who had brought this trouble upon him!

One day he summoned Obadiah, one of the officers of his court. (You remember Obadiah, who feared the Lord and hid the hunted prophets in the caves.) "Let us go through the whole land," said the king, "looking for any streams or water-springs that may yet remain." So they set off. Suddenly on his road Obadiah saw the well-remembered figure of him whom all men were seeking. Prostrate he falls before him.

"Is it thou, my lord Elijah?"

"It is I. Go tell thy lord behold Elijah is here."

Obadiah was astonished and frightened. He knew the danger that Elijah was in. He thought that he would vanish in a moment as he had done before. But Elijah had a great plan in his mind and was determined to meet the king. "No!" said Elijah. "I will not vanish. As the Lord of Hosts liveth before whom I stand I will surely show myself to Ahab to-day."

So the king came, and as he saw the stern prophet standing in his path, and as he thought of these terrible years of famine and drought, fierce anger rose within him.

"Is that you," he cried, "you troubler of Israel?" But Elijah was in no way afraid of him. Sternly he flung back the retort in the teeth of the king. "I am no troubler of Israel," he said, "but thou and thy father's house. You are the troublers who have brought this punishment on Israel; ye have forsaken the commandments of the Lord and thou hast followed Baalim."

And then that lonely prophet challenges that powerful king to a trial of strength. It was to be a contest between Ahab and Elijah, but far more, it was to be a contest between Baal and Jehovah.

It is grand to hear the prophet issuing his orders as if he were the master and Ahab his slave. It is the grandeur of a man who feels sure that God is at his back.

It is the grandeur that in some degree is in every great soul to whom the supreme care is God and the Right, in whom there is no fear except the fear of doing wrong.

"Gather to me all Israel unto Mount Carmel to see the contest. Bring the prophets of Baal, four hundred and fifty, and the four hundred prophets of Ashtoreth who eat at Jezebel's table. And let me stand alone to face them in the name of God!"

I wonder why Ahab obeyed. Perhaps he was afraid of Elijah, or he hoped that he would bring the rain, or he was curious to see the result of the contest. Ahab's was not a strong will. Elijah had caught him when Jezebel was away. The strong fierce queen might have changed the whole position. Ahab consented. He sent for representatives of the tribes to meet him on the appointed day in the wilds of Carmel. He sent to the prophets of Baal and they came. He sent to the prophets at Jezebel's table and they did not come. I dare say the queen prevented them.

For days together all over the Northern Kingdom there was wonder and excitement. Over all the roads the representatives of the nation were crowding to Mount Carmel. The air was electric with the coming storm. It was a time never to be forgotten in Israel.

§ 2. *The Contest on Carmel*

The day of the contest. Early morning. An upland plain upon Mount Carmel. A great crowd. The king and his officers, the thousands of Israel, the four hundred and fifty prophets of Baal in their splendid robes. Straight opposite them, standing alone, the fierce prophet of the Lord in his rough sheepskin cloak.[1]

All hearts are throbbing with excitement. They can see before them the great plain on which most of the old historic battles were fought. They are waiting for a more important battle to-day. Suddenly the tense silence is broken. Elijah is addressing the crowds of Israel. "How long halt ye between two opinions? If the Lord be God, follow him. If Baal, then follow him!"

No answer. "The people answered him not a word." Then the challenge rang out. What was it?

"Here am I alone, a prophet of the Lord. There are the prophets of Baal, four hundred and fifty men. Let them build an altar and place a sacrifice to Baal, but put no fire under. Then let me build an altar and place a sacrifice to Jehovah, but put no fire under. Let both sides cry aloud to heaven that the fire should come down, and the God that answereth by fire let him be God."

Does not it look a very fair challenge? I don't think the prophets of Baal much liked it. But it caught on at once to the people, and from that great assembly came the applauding shout, "It is fair! It is fair!" "It is well spoken."

Then began the great contest, the best known act I suppose in the whole drama of history. First the idol prophets built their altar, and placed their bullock. Then

[1] Stanley, "Jewish Church."

they begin the prayer to their god Baal, the sun-god rolling in the hot heavens above. But no fire comes. Then the prayer grows more eager and excited, *"O Baal, hear us! O Baal, hear us!"* No answer. An hour has elapsed. Another hour. The crowd is growing impatient. More and more excited grow the prayers. It is noon. Their god is nearing the zenith of the sky. Still no answer. Then the prophets go wild with their excitement. They shout and scream and gash themselves with knives and leap like demons on the altar they have made. All in vain.

Then Elijah in his fierce delight begins to mock and laugh at them. "Go on! Go on! Cry louder! Cry louder! for he surely is a god. Perhaps he is thinking. Perhaps he is out walking. Perhaps he is asleep, and needs to be awaked!" You may be sure the people joined in the laugh. You may trust a crowd always to do that. Then the idol prophets went mad with their excitement, screaming and shouting and leaping and gashing themselves till they were all smeared with blood, till they fell down exhausted with the terrible strain.

§ 3. Christ and Elijah

Then calmly, solemnly, Elijah stands forth. He builds his altar, he lays his sacrifice. He orders barrels of water from the well to be poured over it all. Then he waits quietly till the time of Evening Prayer—the time of the offering of the evening sacrifice in the temple. And it came to pass at the time of the offering of the evening sacrifice, that Elijah the prophet came near and said,

"O Lord, the God of Abraham, of Isaac, of Israel, hear me, O Lord, hear me, that this people may know that Thou, Lord, art God, and that Thou hast turned their hearts back again!"

Then fell the lightning of God out of heaven, in a moment, and the excitement of that vast crowd burst forth into one mighty shout, "The Lord He is the God! The Lord He is the God."

It was a great triumph. It was a great lesson, a great warning to that apostate people. The prophet of the Lord was now the master of the whole situation. He was a very fierce, stern prophet. He was greatly angry at the wickedness of the Baal worship. "Take the prophets of Baal," he cried, "let not one of them escape." And they took them, and he brought them down to the brook Kishon, and slew them there.

Was he right in this slaughter? Surely not. Why then does not the Bible blame him for it? I think because he was not much to blame. He did not know any better. He was very jealous for God and for righteousness. He had risked his life unhesitatingly for the right. But the fuller light had not yet come to the world. Jesus Christ had not come.

I have already showed you repeatedly in the past history how gradually God educated mankind. The world is a great gradual school of God. The men of the early ages were like children in the lower classes. Even prophets like Elijah and Deborah did not know as much about God's real will as some of you children in this

Christian land to-day. Therefore we don't blame them for the evil, and we greatly praise them for their good.

Whenever you have doubt about any action of a good man in Old Testament story, bring it to the standard of our Lord.

His disciples once asked Him to let them follow Elijah's example in bringing vengeance on His enemies. You remember how He reproved them? (Luke ix. 54). The spirit of Elijah is not the spirit of Christ. "Ye know not what manner of spirit ye are of."

§ 4. *The Rain*

Now the curse is lifted from the land. The terrible drought and famine shall cease. As the weary, excited crowds are moving aimlessly or preparing to depart, a new sensation comes thrilling amongst them. For Elijah has said unto Ahab, "Get thee up, eat and drink, for there is the sound of the treading of rain." (i.e., the sound of rain-drops as if marching). You can never realize in this country all that that meant to the famine-stricken nation. Green grass, healthy cattle, abundant food, cheap markets, a happy, rejoicing people.

So Ahab went up to eat and drink, and Elijah went up to the top of Carmel. And he bowed himself to the ground, and put his face between his knees in prayer and expectation. And he said to his servant, probably one of the sons of the prophets, perhaps young Jonah, the widow's son, "Go up now, look towards the sea." (the Mediterranean). And he went up and looked, and said, "There is nothing." And he said, "Go again seven times." And it came to pass at the seventh time that he said, "Behold, there ariseth a cloud out of the sea as small as a man's hand."

Before an hour had passed the sky was black with clouds, and the glorious storm wind was rushing through the trees, and there was a great rain. A great, glad, beautiful rain that set the whole land rejoicing. And Ahab drove his chariot exultingly through the storm, and Elijah with his loins girded ran before him to the gate of Jezreel. No farther than the gate, you may be sure, for Jezebel the Queen was inside.

Thus did the providence of God teach a wonderful lesson to Israel. Thus did the kindness of God forgive them and remove their punishment.

(Read 1 Kings xviii.)

QUESTIONS FOR LESSON XI

Tell of Elijah's meeting with Obadiah.

Then tell of his meeting with King Ahab.

What was Elijah's great challenge to Ahab and the prophets of Baal?

Where did the great meeting take place?

Tell the story of it:

(1) Elijah's challenge.

(2) The false prophets' actions.

(3) Elijah's prayer.

(4) What happened.

Tell the story of the coming of the rain.

AHAB AND ELIJAH, PART III

Parts of 1 Kings XIX., XXI., XXII. 34.

2 Kings IX. 30.

§ 1. Elijah "Went for His Life"

The last chapter told of the great triumph of Elijah over Ahab, and over the people, and over the prophets of Baal. And over Jezebel, too, perhaps you would say? Not a bit of it. Jezebel was not of the kind to let any one triumph over her. That night as the rain pattered on the roof and the people in the city shouted their rejoicings, Ahab told the queen the whole story of Elijah and the prophets of Baal on Mount Carmel. You may guess how she listened to that wonderful story. But when he came to the end, and told of her four hundred and fifty prophets of Baal slaughtered by the river-side, the rage of the queen could no longer be controlled. She swore by the gods of her own land that she would have revenge. And she sent a messenger to Elijah to tell him. "May the curse of the gods come on me if I don't

127

make you as dead as one of these prophets by this time to-morrow."

I don't wonder that her husband was afraid of her. I think she for the time frightened even Elijah. When he heard her message, we are told, "he went for his life" away to the wilderness. I do not quite understand this. I do not like to believe that he was afraid, and ran away from his duty. It is hard to believe that of the daring prophet who had stood alone on Carmel against Ahab and the nation and the prophets of Baal. Yet I see "he went for his life." And I see too, I think, that a great and splendid duty lay before him if he had stayed. He had already broken the power of Baal. Ahab was afraid of him. The people were on his side, and it would seem wanted only the presence of a great daring leader to sweep away the idol-worship from the land. It seems such a great pity that he should flee away just then.

It is hard to understand. But I know there are some times in a man's life when he is especially likely to be despondent and afraid. After a great exciting effort there often comes a reaction. A general after the strain of a great battle, a statesman after the strain of a great contest, a preacher after the strain of a great sermon, frequently in the reaction of his feelings falls into deep despondency. Elijah had had the terrible strain of the contest on Carmel and the executing of the Baal prophets. Perhaps that was why he got despondent and afraid just then. Poor Elijah! you see he was but an ordinary man after all. But ordinary men who cling close to God get power to play the hero. Even ordinary people like us.

He sat down under a juniper tree in deep despondency. "Lord, let me die, for I am no better than my fathers." Sometimes people pray that prayer. But God knows best when it is wise to let them die. And don't you think when God has given us a work to do to help Him in pulling the world straight, it is cowardly to want to die and rest? It is like a sentry crying to the captain to let him off duty.

At any rate, God did not let him die. But while he moped and mourned, the word of the Lord came in his heart, "What doest thou here, Elijah?" I think Elijah had no right to be there idling and moping. "I have been very zealous for the Lord of hosts," he replies, "but everybody is gone wrong, the children of Israel have forsaken the Lord and killed his prophets, and I only am left, and they seek my life to take it away."

But the Lord roused him out of this moping and despondency. First He sent him to anoint two kings, Jehu and Hazael, also to anoint Elisha to be a prophet in his stead. And, second, the Lord taught him that things were not at all as bad as he thought, for that there were 7,000 in Israel who had not bowed to Baal. Many good men who, like Elijah, have lost heart about the world, find out, like him, that God was helping it more than they knew. They think that carelessness, and drunkenness, and sin of many kinds are crushing out all good. And then some day God shows them what a great many people more than they know are faithful to Him. God is minding the world a good deal better than some people think.

For some time after this Elijah is lost to our view, until the news of a deed of cruel treachery roused him to face Ahab once more.

§ 2. Naboth's Field

King Ahab had a beautiful palace in Jezreel. I suppose the ivory house was there that we read of in 1 Kings xxii. 39. And he seems to have taken great interest in his palace grounds, and liked to improve and beautify and enlarge them. A very nice taste for any man to have if only he did not do wrong to gratify it.

Now there was a rich vineyard on the hill slope beside the palace grounds, and Ahab thought what a very nice addition it would make to his grounds. He made plans as to what he would do with it. It would just do nicely for a herb garden for the palace. Just the thing to complete his estate. So he went to buy it from Naboth, "I want it very much," said he, "as it is just beside my grounds. I will give you another vineyard for it or I will buy it for money."

"No, you will not," said Naboth, "for I will not sell it at all. It is our family inheritance. God forbid that I should part with it."

Ahab saw that he must give it up, and he went home very cross and disturbed about it. He had so set his heart on that bit of ground. And now he could not have it. What a fool he was, with all his beautiful possessions to fret so much about this. He actually went to bed and turned his face to the wall and would not eat his dinner. It seems very childish, but a good many people act like him still.

But somebody else in the palace had very different notions. "What is the matter with you," asked the queen, "that you will not come to dinner?" "Naboth will not sell me the field that I want so much."

"Will not sell you the field! Are you not the king? Make him do it at once! You say you cannot? Well, soon make him do it. Go and eat your dinner, and let your heart be happy. I will see that you get Naboth's field."

I don't think Ahab knew what she intended. But he was guilty all the same, for he might have guessed that she would stop at nothing. When he was gone she went and got the king's letter paper and the king's seal, and wrote a letter in the king's name to the chiefs of Naboth's village:—

"Arrange a religious service. Bring in Naboth. Then suddenly make a false charge against him and pay two wicked men to tell lies and say that they heard him cursing God and the King. Then take him out and stone him."

What an awfully wicked thing to write! Did they obey? Yes. They, like everyone else, were afraid of the queen. The cowardly judges brought in that poor, honest farmer, and got those lies told, and then took out Naboth to be stoned. Then as he lay there, battered dead with stones, they wrote to Jezebel that the deed was done. And Jezebel told Ahab that he might now take possession of the field.

§ 3. Retribution

I suppose the report got about. At any rate it somehow reached Elijah. And in his fierce indignation at the cruel wrong he felt the voice of God in his heart telling him what he should do. The despondency and cowardice were all gone now. He must face the wicked king whatever the result.

So when Ahab came down to take possession of his new garden, an ugly surprise was in store for him. I can fancy him walking up and down gloating over his possession, planning how to improve it and fit it for his purpose. Suddenly a shadow lies across his path and he hears a harsh, stern voice beside him. "Hast thou killed and also taken possession?" The king's guilty conscience made this sore to bear.

"Hast thou found me, O mine enemy?" cried the king.

"Yes," said Elijah, "I have found thee, because thou hast sold thyself to work evil in the sight of the Lord. Now thus saith the Lord, In the place where dogs licked the blood of Naboth shall the dogs lick thy blood, even thine. And of Jezebel also thus saith the Lord, The dogs shall eat Jezebel by the rampart of Jezreel." What an awful sentence upon them both!

*   *   *   *   *   *   *   *

Years afterwards I can see Ahab in his war-chariot at the end of a battle, with a deep wound bleeding inside his armour. "And at even the king died, and the blood ran out of the wound into the bottom of the chariot. So they brought him to Samaria, and they washed the chariot by the pool of Samaria, and the dogs licked up his blood." (1 Kings xxii. 38).

$$*\quad *\quad *\quad *\quad *\quad *\quad *\quad *$$

Years afterwards again I see the palace of Jezreel, and the widowed Queen Jezebel looking out of an upper window. She is speaking with anger to a warrior below, Jehu, the son of Nimshi, who had just slain her son. "Who is on my side?" cried Jehu; "throw her down!" So they threw her down, and some of her blood was sprinkled on the wall and on the horses, and he trod her under foot. And by-and-by, when they went to bury her, they found that the wild dogs had eaten her and left "no more than the skull and the feet and the palms of her hands."

Such was the fate Ahab and Jezebel brought on themselves by their wickedness.

(Read 1 Kings xix., xxi., xxii. 34; 2 Kings ix. 30.)

QUESTIONS FOR LESSON XII

Why did Elijah run away and hide?

How was he called back?

Tell the story of Naboth's vineyard.

Was God angry at this awful crime?

Tell of Elijah's meeting with Ahab after it and the terrible doom pronounced on Ahab and Jezebel.

Tell how their punishment came.

LESSON XIII

ELISHA AND THE
HOUSE OF JEHU

The necessary parts of 2 Kings II., IV., V.

§ 1. Elijah's Departure

You remember when Elijah was moping and desponding in the wilderness the Lord sent him to anoint Jehu as king instead of Ahab, and Elisha as prophet instead of himself. Elijah and Ahab had finished their parts. They were to be succeeded by Elisha and Jehu. Thus the world goes on. We do not know how long Elijah lived after pronouncing Ahab's doom that day in the field of Naboth. He seems to have retired again away into the wilderness.

Then suddenly there comes into the history the story of Elijah's last day on earth. His work was done in this world, and the Lord had need of him in the other life. I suppose he had been thinking and praying all night and then early in the morning he started off with Elisha to walk the round of the old places where he had worshipped God, Gilgal and Bethel and Jericho. I think as they went he told Elisha what was to happen, so it was a very solemn walk for them both. When they came to Bethel they found waiting for them the young students, "sons of the prophets," who had a sort of divinity school there for learning about God. They knew that they were seeing their great teacher for the last time, and they talked with Elisha about it. "Ah, I know it!" said he, "hold ye your peace." "Don't come further with me," said Elijah to him, "the Lord is sending me on to Jericho—on to Jordan." "Nay," said Elisha, "as the Lord liveth I will not leave thee." And so at each stopping place Elijah trying to go alone, Elisha pressing sorrowfully on to see the last of his dear master.

"So they two went on." It reminds me of the departure of Moses to die, only that Moses went altogether alone. Suddenly some very startling thing happened. A great, raging storm seems to have swept down from the mountains, a mighty whirlwind, and I suppose thunder and lightning. And then the story says "there appeared a chariot of fire and horses of fire, and Elijah went up by a whirlwind to heaven." That is all. How much it means we do not know. "They sought for him three days and found him not." They never found him again. The belief was that he had been carried off to heaven without dying.

At any rate he passed into that Paradise life where all the noble souls of the old world awaited him. And I can fancy him meeting Moses there and Joshua and David, and learning with them more of God's great plans for Israel and for the world. I can fancy them watching with wondering hearts as they saw Christ come to earth, and learned the full meaning of the love of God. This is not any mere fancy of mine. You remember how it is proved in later history? Yes. When Moses and Elijah, the two most eager and impetuous of them all, burst forth out of that Kingdom to talk to our Lord on the mount of Transfiguration about "his decease which he should accomplish at Jerusalem." Ah, I think that world is very close to us, and God's servants there are watching with deep interest always God's plans for the world.

§ 2. Stories of Elisha

Elisha has to remain on earth. God has much for him to do before he is free to follow his master. He must watch over Israel and warn the kings and preach God's will to the people. He was not as fierce and stern as Elijah. He lived a much quieter life, and the kings were more respectful and more friendly to him. But I think he could be just as fearless and firm as Elijah when it was necessary. There are all sorts of nice kindly stories told about him.

The men of his city told him how bad the water in their wells was, and he sweetened it by a miracle (2 Kings ii. 19). The widow of a prophet came crying to him that she had no money to pay her dead husband's debts, and that his creditors would carry off her two children as slaves. "Go and borrow all the vessels that you can," said Elisha. Then he prayed to God and by a miracle filled the vessels with costly oil, and so she paid her debt (2 Kings iv. 1).

A kindly Shunamite woman made a chamber for him, with a bed, a table, a stool, and a candlestick, so that he could sleep there when passing that way. She greatly longed to have a son, and he prayed to God to send her a little baby. By-and-by she came to him in terrible trouble. Her son was dead. Elisha was very, very sorry, and he prayed earnestly to God. But the child did not rise. Then he went in and shut the door of the room and prayed very earnestly, and stretched himself on the dead boy. But still he was dead. Then he prayed still more, walking up and down. At last the child opened his eyes and sneezed! And he was very glad to give the woman her son.

Another time an axe-head fell off and sank in the water and he restored it. Another time the food in a pot was accidentally poisoned and he made it right (2 Kings iv. 38; vi. 5).

Amongst all these kindly stories is one horrible one, which I cannot understand at all. It says that he made bears come out of a wood to devour some lads who called him "old baldhead." If he really did this, either it was very wicked of him or else there must have been some reason that we do not know of. But it is not at all in keeping with the kindly things we know about him. You see there must have been a great many legends floating about with regard to a great man like Elisha.

§ 3. Spiritual Guardians

There are two stories about him that I must not pass over. One night he was sleeping in a little place called Dothan. You remember it before? Yes; it was the place where Joseph's brethren sold him (Genesis xxxvii. 17). Well, when Elisha's servant awoke and looked out in the morning he got a great fright. All around the little town was a host of soldiers with horses and chariots sent by the King of Syria to capture the prophet! In terror the servant rushed in, "O Master, what shall we do?" Elisha looked up quite calmly. "Fear not, they that be with us are more than those against us."

You see men who believe greatly in God do not get frightened easily. Then he prayed, "Lord, open his eyes." And when the young man looked again he saw a vision on the mountains around of horses and chariots of fire guiding Elisha. That means that if we were able to see spiritual things we should see how close God and His care and His power is all around us. It is just as true even though we do not see it. In another life I suppose we shall have power to see this always. But it is just as real now. I suppose that was why Elisha saw nothing strange in the idea of Elijah's being carried off to heaven by chariots of God.

Then, the story says, he prayed to God to make the Syrian soldiers blind for a time, and then he led them blindly into the presence of their enemy, the King of Israel. Then he restored their sight. What a fright they must have got! "My father!" cried the king. "Shall I kill them?" "Certainly not," said Elisha; "give them a good dinner and let them go back to their master." I think the king of Syria must have thought a great deal better of Elisha and of God after that.

§ 4. Naaman the Leper

Soon afterwards he had still more reason to think well of him. The story of Naaman is told before this, but it probably occurred later. Naaman was a great officer in the Syrian army. The Jews used to think that it was he who shot Ahab in battle. A great officer and a great favourite of the King, one would think he ought to have been very happy. But there had come to him a terrible trouble—a terrible secret trouble that he concealed from every one as long as he could. Under his beautiful uniform and his golden armour his wife knew that the ugly white blotches of leprosy were on his skin and some day it would kill him. So the great soldier whom men bowed down before went about his duties with a hopeless, sorrowful heart. By-and-by it grew worse, I suppose it appeared on his face. It became known.

At this time Jehu was king of Israel, and there were continual battles between Syria and Israel. Perhaps after one of these battles, or after the battle in which Ahab was killed, Naaman had brought home all his captives as slaves, and it seems that he had given a little Israelite girl to his wife to be her maid. She soon learned the terrible secret that her mistress was fretting over. I think she was very fond of her mistress, and one day she ventured to say to her, "Oh, I wish the master were with our great prophet in Samaria. I am sure he could cure him."

*   *   *   *   *   *   *   *

The Syrian chariots and horses are again round about the house of Elisha. Not to capture or hurt him though this time. The great Syrian general is waiting at the door with all his company, and with his bags of silver for reward. He wants the prophet to cure him of his leprosy. He waits and waits, but no Elisha. He is getting impatient. At last Elisha's servant comes out, "Go and wash in Jordan seven times." That is all. Naaman is furious at such neglect. To send a mere servant to the great lord of Syria! To tell him to go and bathe in their beggarly little Jewish river! So he turned and went away in a rage. Very foolish, don't you think? His officers thought so too. So they pleaded with him, and at last he gave in. He turned his chariots and drove to the Jordan. How anxious he was! How excited they all were as the leper went down into the river. He plunged in. Once. No change. Twice. No change. Again and again and again, with the dread and the hope struggling in his heart. Once more! Seventh time! Oh, his flesh is as clean and smooth as the flesh of a little child! The leper is cured!

Wild with delight he drives back to Elisha. "Oh, your God is the true God. I will never worship idols again." Then he offered rich rewards to Elisha. But he would not touch them. I suppose he thought it would bring more honour to God and to true religion if he refused to take rewards. So Naaman talked with him about his future and how he might be faithful to God in a heathen land. And then he departed for Syria.

A beautiful story so far. Now comes a very ugly part. The servant of the prophet was probably training to be a prophet himself. But he was a very covetous man. He looked greedily at the rich presents that Elisha refused. He watched them disappearing in the treasure chariots over the hill. He must have known that Elisha had good reason for refusing them. Then the evil thought came to him and he stole softly out till he was out of sight of the house and then ran fast after Naaman's chariot. "The prophet sent me after you, my lord; he wants some money to give to two young strangers just come to him." I fancy Naaman thought a little less of Elisha and his religion when he heard this. But he gladly gave Gehazi twice what he asked, and he stole home guiltily and hid it. Then he appeared before his master. And Elisha asked, "Where have you been, Gehazi?" "Nowhere? did not my heart go with you when the man turned back in his chariot to meet you?" Elisha was very angry. "The leprosy therefore of Naaman shall cleave unto thee and to thy seed for ever." And he went out from his presence a leper as white as snow. I wonder if Naaman ever heard the truth of that story.

§ 5. *Death of Elisha*

Elisha lived for a long time and had great influence for good with the kings and with the nation. He saw the punishment fall on the house of Ahab. He knew when Ahab's blood was licked by the dogs at the pool of Samaria. He saw Ahab's sons succeed him on the throne. Then he fulfilled the charge left him by Elijah, to anoint "Jehu the son of Nimshi, the furious chariot driver," to be king.

Jehu was a fierce cruel king. He killed in cold blood the sons of Ahab. He trampled the body of Queen Jezebel under his horses' feet. However much Ahab's family may have deserved their fate, we can only think with horror of the cruel Jehu as we think of the hangman who hangs the criminal. Elisha had a very wicked, wretched time to live through. It would probably have been much worse if he had not been there. At last he died, honoured and mourned, and was buried in a grand tomb in Samaria, and long afterwards it was rumoured that miracles were wrought by his bones (2 Kings xiii. 21).

(Read the necessary parts of 2 Kings ii., iv., v.)

QUESTIONS FOR LESSON XIII

What is the Israelite story of Elijah's departure from earth?

Did he ever come back to earth from the Other World?

Who was the new prophet who succeeded him?

Tell of the visions of horses and chariots from the Other World.

Do you think that Other World is always around us and observing us?

Can we see them?

Our Lord tells of guardian angels watching the children on earth and of joy in heaven over one sinner that repenteth. What does that lead us to think about that other world watching us?

Tell briefly the story of Naaman.

JEROBOAM THE GREAT AND HIS THREE GREAT PROPHETS

2 Kings XIV. 23, 24 and parts of

prophecies of Jonah and Amos.

After Jehu came his son Jehoahaz, and after him came his son Joash to the throne of Israel. There is not much good to say of either of them. On the death of Joash came his son Jeroboam the Great, a much more able man than either of his two predecessors. His victories soon made his name famous, and brought much wealth and luxury and glory to Israel. But it was a bad time in spite of all. The people were very prosperous and very successful and very wicked. The king after his long reign of forty years gets this epitaph in the Bible, "He did that which was evil in the sight of the Lord, and departed not from all the sins of Jeroboam the son of Nebat, wherewith he made Israel to sin."

§ 1. *Jonah*

So you will easily see the need of God sending His prophets in that gay, prosperous, wicked time. The first whom we hear of is Jonah, the son of Amittai. We have all heard of him in that very strange story of "Jonah and the whale," which is told in the history of his visit to Nineveh. We really do not know much about him.

I told you earlier that there was a Jewish tradition that he was the boy of Zarepta, whom Elijah restored to life and who followed the old prophet into the wilderness. Whether this be so or not, at any rate he prophesied in the time of Jeroboam the Great. His prophecies are all lost except one recorded in 2 Kings xiv. 25, telling of the success that Jeroboam would win for Israel. I wish we could get hold of these lost prophecies, and find out what he said to keep Israel from sin. I think they would be different from other prophecies. If the Jewish tradition is true, he was not a Jew at all, and therefore he would probably have broader notions than the Jewish prophets. Some of them seem to have thought that God cared for the Jews only. I do not know what Jonah thought, but it is beautiful to see him stirred by the Spirit of God to go away outside his own land, to preach to the great city of Nineveh, the city of the Assyrian enemy. (Read here part of Jonah i.) It must have helped to teach his nation that God cared for every poor child of man, even the enemies of Israel. For the Lord said, "Should not I have pity on Nineveh, that great city, wherein are more than six-score thousand persons that cannot discern between their right hand and their left, and also much cattle?"

I like to think of this beautiful lesson about God. I should think it was because of this that Jonah's history got into the Bible, in spite of the story of the big fish that swallowed him. I do not myself believe that that really happened. God could and did do far more wonderful miracles. But it looks very improbable. Some very thoughtful writers believe that it was never intended as a real story but as a striking parable prophesying the future fate of Israel. Quite probably that is the truth. But we really know nothing about it. I think the common people at any rate took it as a real story. Maybe it was a misunderstanding of something that really happened. I know some very good people who think it quite impossible that anything not absolutely true could have got into the Bible. But it is not quite impossible, and the Bible does not anywhere make such a claim. That story of Jonah's would not be written for years after, but passed on by word of mouth in Nineveh and in Samaria, in the villages and in the country places, and among the sailors in Tarshish. It would be quite easy for additions to creep into the story. No doubt Jonah was miraculously saved by God. Suppose he was picked up by a boat called *The Whale* or *The Fish*, and that the story of his rescue floated about for years amongst ignorant people, some story like this might easily arise. When the Jewish Church was guided in later years by God to see the beautiful lesson of His love in Jonah's story, they would put it into their collection of Scriptures. The incident of the Big Fish was in it. Probably they believed it to be true. Or, perhaps they did not like to meddle with the story as it was told in

147

their day. At any rate, the story of God sending Jonah to Nineveh was true, and the great lesson of God's love was true. That was what really mattered. I do not feel quite certain that every statement of the number of soldiers or of horses or chariots in the Bible is absolutely accurate. Just like other historians, the historians of the Bible had to learn their facts from others, or from their own observation, and God worked no miracle to save them from mistakes. God's guidance only taught them to teach true lessons about the facts that they knew of God's dealings with men.

I wonder if we shall ever find those lost prophecies of Jonah. I wonder if they would help us to understand about the whale. I wish we knew more about him and his intercourse with the king.

§ 2. Amos

But there was another prophet of whom we know more and who teaches us a great deal of the state of society at the time. For happily his prophecies have not got lost. Though indeed they might almost as well have, for all the use that we make of them.

You know that set of short books at the end of the Old Testament, Joel and Amos and Nahum and Micah and the others, all thrown together as it were in a heap, as if we did not know what to do with them. I think it would be a good thing if we could arrange the books of the Bible in their right places. I should like to see these prophets put with their right kings. These prophecies piled up in a heap belong to quite different times and places, and of course people do not understand them when they are out of their right times and places. Suppose you got a collection of English national speeches made in the reigns of James I. and Queen Victoria, and Oliver Cromwell and King Alfred, and William the Conqueror and Richard of the Lion Heart—speeches all mixed up in one collection with nothing to tell you what time they were spoken, how confusing it would be! And what new interest would come into English history if we could read them in their right places. Now this is what I want you to get the habit of doing with the prophets of Israel and Judah.

Open your Bible at the Book of Amos. It begins by telling you that he prophesied in the days of Uzziah, King of Judah, and of Jeroboam the Great, of Israel, two years before the Great Earthquake (Amos i. 1, 2). Now we see where we are. We do not know enough about the history to understand all that he is thinking of, but at any rate he will throw much light on the history. It is listening to the words of a man who was there at the time, and walked those streets, and saw those sins, and knew the king, and the priests, and the chief of the people. When you read his whole prophecy you will find out that he belonged to the other Kingdom, of Judah—that he was not a regular prophet, but a poor countryman, a sort of farm labourer, preparing the coarse figs for cattle. I suppose that is why his visions are so much about country things, vineyards and fig-trees, and fruit baskets, and wagons and corn and such things.

A countryman, you see, would get a good deal of

149

time for thinking and meditating, and a thoughtful religious man would learn much about God and the Bible, and the fate of the nation in all his quiet years in the fields. So it was with Abraham and Moses and David long before. This man could not rest in his anxiety about the nation. He was so accustomed to think of God acting continually in the world that he felt it was God's call. "The Lord said unto me, Go, prophesy to my people Israel." So he went off all the way to Samaria with the great burden of God's message on his heart.

§ 3. "Reprove, Exhort, Rebuke"

One wonders how a poor country labourer would have any influence with rich, powerful, grand people. But somehow a man that feels very deeply God's presence, and is terribly in earnest about righteousness, always is listened to. Amos, like Jonah, knows that God cares for people outside Israel. The first prophecies in the book are against outside nations, Damascus and Gaza and Tyre and Edom, not because of idolatry or faults of worship, but because they had been unfair or unkind or dishonourable. He felt that God must punish these things everywhere and always. But I think these prophecies were before he came up to preach against Israel.

When he comes to Israel he is very stern. "They sell the righteous for silver, and the poor for a pair of shoes. They afflict the just, they take a bribe. They know not to do right, saith the Lord God." Their drunkenness is a disgrace, he says, even in the palace. He is specially fierce with the great ladies of the court and the city for drunkenness and vice, and oppression of the poor. "Ye cows of Bashan, who oppress the poor and crush the needy, and say unto your husbands, Bring drink and let us drink." He notices all the luxury and grandeur of that prosperous time, the great houses and palaces of hewn stone, the ivory beds, the silken cushions, the idle songs to the harp and the viol. God, he says, "will smite the winter house with the summer house, and the houses of ivory shall perish." They boast of their festivals and Church worship. "I hate, I despise your feast days, saith the Lord, I will not smell in your solemn assemblies. Though you offer burnt offerings I will not accept them, nor regard your peace offerings." "Thus saith the Lord, Wailing shall be in all the broad ways, and they shall say in all the streets, Alas! alas!" And then comes the definite terrible threat of the captivity. "Therefore will I cause you to go into captivity beyond Damascus, saith the Lord, whose name is The God of hosts." (ch. v. 27). "The sanctuaries of Israel shall be laid waste, saith the Lord, and I will rise against the house of Jeroboam with the sword." (ch. vii. 9).

One does not wonder that wicked, godless people should get angry at this plain speaking. Amaziah, the priest of the golden calves at Bethel, sent a complaint to the king, "Amos hath conspired against thee, for thus saith Amos, Jeroboam shall die by the sword, and Israel shall surely be led captive out of his land." "Get out of this to your own country," he said to Amos. "You have no business coming here from Judah to prophesy in the king's chapel."

So Amos had to go. And all the wickedness went on as before. Another prophet, Hosea, arose soon after, but he also failed. We shall hear of him later on. So you see the great King Jeroboam II., with all his grandeur, and all his victories, had a bad enough time in his old age. He could not forget what these prophets had threatened, and some of the enemies on his borders made him feel that the threats might come true. However, he died peacefully himself before the great troubles came. We shall learn more of them in the next chapter.

(Read 2 Kings xiv. 23, and parts of the prophecies of Jonah and Amos.)

QUESTIONS FOR LESSON XIV

Who was the great King of Israel now?

Who were the three great prophets?

Find in the Bible their books of sermons and speeches.

Why was Jonah sent to Nineveh?

What are we to think about this story of Jonah and the whale?

What do we know of Amos?

What should people do before reading the books of these prophets? *Answer*: They should go back to this history and learn about their surroundings.

THE PROPHET HOSEA AND THE FALL OF ISRAEL

Parts of Hosea V, and 2 Kings referred to.

§ 1. Growing Worse and Worse

After the riches and prosperity and victories and deep, dark sin of the reign of King Jeroboam II., the history of Israel is all sad and full of trouble to the end. You remember the stern words of the prophet Amos against the sins of the people, and his prophecy that punishment should certainly come—then his more clear and definite threat, "Therefore ye shall go into captivity with the first that go captive" (Amos vi. 1, etc.). I do not think the people believed him. Somehow they thought that if they went to church regularly and offered sacrifices and went through their little round of ceremonies that God would be satisfied. Would He? What did God really want above everything else? Yes. Righteousness. That His people should be true and honest and generous and loving. That they should be faithful to their God and loving to their brethren. Very patiently God waited after the stern warnings of Amos. But the people would not believe nor give up their wickedness. So the terrible days of captivity and ruin had to come.

After the great King Jeroboam II. died, his son Zechariah was made king, but after a few months a conspiracy was formed by his officers, and when the young king was feasting in the night they murdered him (2 Kings xv. 10; Hosea vii. 5-7). So ended the whole race of Jehu in the fourth generation, according to the word of the Lord.

Shallum, chief of the conspirators, became king. Very soon came another conspiracy, and Shallum was murdered. And so it went on for about fifty years. Battles and conspiracies and murders, and one wicked king following another till one gets sick of the wretched story, and feels that there was nothing else to do with Israel but to sweep it away altogether.

§ 2. Hosea's Training

Had God forgotten this sinning people all this time? No. He never forgets. He still watched over them with deep pain at their sin. Did you ever think of the deep eternal pain that must be in God's heart at the sins of men? I think if we knew how much He cares we should try harder to stop paining Him.

Now something happened in Israel that often happens, and that to careless people might seem all chance. There was a man of Israel named Hosea. He was a good, loving-hearted man, very sorry for the state of his country. I do not think he was one of the prophets until his troubles made him one. He married Gomer, the daughter of Diblaim. He loved her very tenderly. But oh! she was a very bad woman. She committed horrible sins that disgraced her family and nearly broke her poor husband's heart. For years and years he bore with her, concealing her vileness and keeping his deep sorrow buried in his own heart. But she only got worse and worse, and at the last she deserted him altogether and went away to live with wicked people. Then it would seem that she fell so low that she was a sort of slave. One would think that Hosea would be sick of her by this time and glad to get rid of her. But no. His heart was still full of tenderness and sorrow for her. He knew that she must be very miserable, and though she had deserved it all, though she had utterly disgraced him, he could not forget her nor forsake her in her misery. So he bought her back to him for fifteen pieces of silver, and let her live in a room in his house. Though he could not take her back as his wife any more, yet he seems to have done all that he could to keep her from her sin and make her better and happier by his tenderness over her.

§ 3. God's Tenderness

I do not believe that this poor, tender, sorrowing husband had any idea at the time that God's good purposes to Israel could be helped by this misery in his life. Yet it was. I told you how troubled he was over his country's sins and dangers. But now as he thought and thought about his own great sorrows, and felt that he could not forget or forsake this wretched, sinful wife, whom he loved, I think it gradually dawned on him that perhaps God's sorrow and love for Israel might be like his own sorrow and love for his wife. The more he thought of it the more strongly he felt it. God's Spirit stamped it on his heart. I can imagine him saying within himself some day, "surely God must be at least as loving and tender as I am. I am but a poor ordinary sinful man, yet I can love and suffer pain at the sin of my wife. I can't cast her off. Surely God is ever so much better than I am. And if so, surely He must have ever so much more love and feel ever so much more pain for the sins of His people."

The Bible says, the word of the Lord came unto Hosea, telling him that like his loving tenderness to his wife was God's loving tenderness to His sinful people. I think this word of the Lord came to him, not by dreams or visions or outward voices, but in the way I have told you, God speaking in his heart. And when he felt quite sure that this was so he saw God's hand in all his troubles. I think he hated talking of them, but since everybody knew, he told with as much reserve as possible just what God had taught him, and I think the people believed more in God's love to them when they knew the terrible way in which Hosea had learned it (Hosea i.-iii.).[1]

---

[1]To any careful reader of Scripture it must be evident that this is the meaning of Hosea's story. To say that God told him for sake of a parable to marry a woman of ill repute would be horrible, and such an act would certainly not make his prophecies more acceptable.

§ 4. God's Pain

A man who felt things as keenly as Hosea must have had a very sorrowful heart about the troubles of his country. He began to prophesy in the days of Jeroboam II. (*ch.* i. 1). He saw the victories and the rejoicings and the outward prosperity, and the brilliant crowds worshipping in the idol temple, and all the wickedness in the gay life of the people. He knew of the murder of the new king, and lived through most of the wretched time of conspiracies and murders and changes of kings that followed. God seemed almost forgotten.

"Hear the word of the Lord," cries the prophet (iv. 1, 2), "because there is no truth nor mercy nor knowledge of God in the land. There is nought but swearing and breaking faith and killing and stealing and committing adultery. They break out, and blood touches blood. Therefore shall the land mourn and every one of the dwellers in it shall languish," etc. And yet through it all you see how sorrowful he is about it. It nearly breaks his heart to think of what is coming. But it is still no use. They will not listen to him. They try to get help everywhere except from God. They turn, he says, to Assyria for help and then to Egypt, "but they turn not to the Lord their God, and seek not Him for all this." Therefore, he says, their captivity must come; the nation shall be swept away. "The Assyrian shall be king over them." But it is very touching to see how his own deep troubles have taught him God's pain about His people. Look at chapter xi., where the prophet represents God speaking, "When Israel was a child I

157

loved him, I called my son out of Egypt, I taught him to walk, I took him in my arms, I drew him with bands of love" . . . But now "the Assyrian shall be his king, because he refuses to return. The sword shall fall upon his cities—my people are bent on backsliding. . . . How shall I give thee up, Ephraim? How shall I cast thee away, Israel? My heart is turned within me, my compassions are kindled together. I will not execute the fierceness of mine anger, for I am God and not man, the Holy One in the midst of thee."

Then in the 14th chapter, the end of his prophecies, he begins, "O Israel, return unto the Lord thy God, for thou hast fallen by thine iniquity." Then he goes on despairing of their repentance, yet looking forward to some day, far away perhaps in the future ages, when hope should still be for that ruined Israel. I wonder if that was St. Paul's thought when he says (Romans xi. 26), that somewhere in the future "all Israel shall be saved."

§ 5. The Ruin of Israel

So you see you must learn to read the prophet Hosea in his right place in the history, then you will understand what he means. I think it is very helpful in the midst of this old chronicle of the Israelite story to get the very words and pleadings of a man living at the time. You see the story in the books of Kings and Chronicles is too short, too condensed, to be interesting. It is gathered from earlier lost histories and only here and there do we get the full colour and life of the old stories left us. In stories such as that of Goliath and

Absalom's death, and Elijah and Ahab, the historian seems to leave the old history as it stood, and it is full of life and interest. So Amos and Hosea coming in here with their living words, put life into this story and make us "put ourselves into the place" of the people of that time.

It was in vain that Amos and Hosea pleaded. The people would not reform. Things went on from bad to worse. A king named Pekahiah was murdered by one Pekah, who then became king. The great king of Assyria came against him and carried off the Israelites of the tribes beyond Jordan (show on map). Thus the long threatened captivity of Israel began (2 Kings xv. 27-32). By-and-by Pekah was murdered by a conspirator named Hoshea, who then became king by the help of the Assyrian enemy, to whom he had to pay tribute. While he kept quiet and paid tribute the Assyrians let him alone. But when his Assyrian conqueror died, several of the subject states tried to rebel. Hoshea thought he saw a chance of setting Israel free, so he asked the help of the King of Egypt and then refused to pay his tribute to Assyria. Then the angry Assyrians swept down in great force upon the country, carried off King Hoshea as a hostage for their tribute money, inflicted great slaughter on the people, and at last laid siege to Samaria, the capital. The Israelites fought bravely for nearly three years; then at last they gave way to despair. The city was stormed. There was a terrible massacre and 27,000 people were carried away into captivity by the Assyrians, perhaps to Nineveh, where Jonah had been sent long ago.

Thus ended the Kingdom of Israel, the Northern Kingdom (2 Kings xvii.). We know nothing more of the exiles who were carried away. There are many silly speculations still about them. People say that the English nation is descended from them. This is all foolishness. They probably soon died or got mixed up with their conquerors, but their country saw them no more. The stern judgment of God had fallen on them for their sins, as it will for ever fall on all evil nations. What God may have in store for them in the far future in the great land beyond the grave we do not know. We can only hope with a vague wonder as to what St. Paul meant—"all Israel shall be saved."

§ 6. The Samaritans

Before we pass on away from this story of Israel, there is an interesting piece of history here that must not be left out. In 2 Kings xvii. 24, etc., we are told that the king of Assyria, after carrying off the Israelites, brought men from Babylon and Cutha and Ava, etc., and placed them in Samaria instead of the Children of Israel. These heathen people got frightened at some attacks of lions, and thought that they had better serve the God of the land along with their own gods. So the Assyrians sent back one of the captive priests to teach them to worship God.

It was a miserable sort of worship (v. 33), "They feared the Lord and served their own gods." By-and-by they married with the remnant of Israelites left in the land, and as time went on they became worshippers of

God and learned a good deal about Him and had their own special copy of the books of Moses, which they were very proud of. These are the Samaritans, of whom you read so much afterwards in our Lord's life. The Jews hated and scorned them. "The Jews have no dealings with the Samaritans," said the Samaritan woman to our Lord. But our Lord was very kind and gentle with them. Do not forget now the difference between the Jews and the Samaritans.

(Read parts of Hosea and of 2 Kings referred to.)

QUESTIONS FOR LESSON XV

Open your Bibles at the Book of Hosea. Tell something about Hosea's wife.

Did he feel sorry for her?

What did this sorrow teach him about God and Israel?

Now comes the fall of this Northern Kingdom of Israel. What happened to it?

Who were the Samaritans that we read of in the New Testament?

SAUL
DAVID
SOLOMON

ISRAEL	JUDAH
Jeroboam	Rehoboam
Nadab	Abejah
Baasha	Asa
Elah	JEHOSAPHAT
Zimri	Jehoram
Omri	Ahaziah
Ahab	Alhabah
Ahaziah	Joash
Jehoram	Amaziah
Jehu	Uzziah
Jehoahaz	Jotham
Jehoash	Ahaz
JEROBOAM II	HEZEKIAH
Zechariah, Shallum,	Manasseh
and Menaher	Amon
Pekarah and Pekah	JOSIAH
Hoshea	Jehoahaz and Jehoiakim
ASSYRIAN CAPTIVITY	Jehoiachin and Zedekiah
	BABYLONIAN CAPTIVITY

PART II

THE STORY OF THE KINGDOM OF JUDAH

The story of the kingdom of Judah now begins. Be clear about the position of things:—

1. After Solomon's death the kingdom was divided into two.

2. The ten tribes of the North formed the kingdom of Israel under Jeroboam.

3. The two tribes of the South remaining faithful to Rehoboam made the southern kingdom of Judah.

4. The kingdom of Israel existed for about 300 years, when the ten tribes were carried into Captivity by the King of Assyria.

5. The kingdom of Judah existed for about 400 years, when it was swept away by Nebuchadnezzar to Babylon.

THE STORY OF SEVEN KINGS AND OF TWO BAD WOMEN

1 Kings XV. 9 etc., and 2 Kings XI.

We are now beginning the history of the kingdom of Judah. We begin it with the story of "the first seven kings." And I am sorry to say the story of the first seven kings is largely the story of two bad women.

§ 1. King Asa and the Bible

We have already had in full the story of the first King Rehoboam at the time of the Division of the Kingdom. He seems not to have been so much wicked as weak and easily led. You will often find that weak people do more harm than wicked people if they get under the control of some one worse than themselves. It is our duty not to be weak in matters of right and wrong. If we are in earnest and ask Him, God will always help us to see the right and make us brave and strong to do it in spite of any risk of being hurt or being laughed at, or even of vexing some one that we are fond of.

Rehoboam was very fond of one of his wives named Maacah, who was a worshipper of the evil gods that Jezebel afterwards worshipped in the North. It was a good thing in him that he should so love her. But it was not a good thing to do wrong in order to please her. Wrong must not be done at any cost or to please anybody. That is the eternal law of God for ever. Rehoboam allowed his queen to lead him into idolatry and all sorts of wrong. It is said of him "he did evil because he fixed not his heart to seek the Lord." He fixed not his heart—he was not strong or determined.

When he died his son Abijah succeeded him, and he was entirely under the rule of his wicked mother, so that things got worse and worse in Jerusalem. By-and-by when Abijah died and his son Asa became king, the old grandmother, who was queen still, wanted to keep on her evil power. But Asa would have none of it. Some body must have taught him religion; it is hard to say who in that very godless home. Perhaps one of the prophets at the court. At any rate, he tried to do God's will. He determined to put down the worship of Baal and all the filthy evil practices connected with it. And before he could do anything in this matter he had to face his grandmother. She had got made "an abominable image,"[1] we are told, for worship. Asa felt that this was a hateful thing in God's sight, so he removed it and burned it. And next he removed its owner from being queen-mother and ruling in the land. There was really nothing else to be done with such a woman. It is a curious fact and rather amusing that the story of this

[1] 1 Kings xv. 13.

removal of the queen-mother had something to do many centuries afterwards with the preparing of our present "Authorised Version" of the Bible. You know it was prepared by order of King James I. of England. The Geneva Bible was the popular Bible before. It had notes in the margin, and at this story of Asa removing the queen-mother the note said, "Herein he showed lack of zeal, for she ought to have died." You remember James's mother, Mary Queen of Scots, had been put to death not long before, and some stupid and bigoted Protestants thought it served her right for wanting to bring back Romanism. So they made this note apply to her. King James was furious, and it was one of the several reasons that got us our best version of the Bible. Strange how God can use all sorts of foolishness of men to get good done!

§ 2. Jehosaphat's Mistake

King Asa did what he could, and though his closing years were not satisfactory, he must get credit for being a good king. He died when Ahab was King of Israel in the North, and then his son Jehosaphat became king in his stead, Jehosaphat was a wise and great and good king, and he kept clear of the idol worship and put it down all over the land. And because he felt that ignorance of God was largely the cause of this evil, in his third year he sent princes and teachers all through the country towns to teach the most ignorant people about the law of God, "And they had the Book of the Law with them, and taught all the people." (2 Chronicles xvii. 7-9).

It is a pleasure to read of all that he did for his country. But he made one very bad mistake, which in after years undid much of this good. Ahab was King of Israel and was very powerful. Jehosaphat was a little afraid of him, so he built cities and castles and forts and put a very strong garrison in Jerusalem. All very good so far. But then instead of doing the right and trusting God for the rest, he thought it would be a great help if he united his family to Ahab's in marriage. So he proposed that the crown prince Jehoram should be married to the princess Athaliah, the daughter of Ahab and Jezebel. This of course made Judah safe against attack from Israel, and it brought some increase of outward prosperity. But it was an awful risk to bring in a daughter of Jezebel into his family. After all that his father had suffered from one bad woman, surely he should have been more careful. I suppose he thought that because the girl was young he could keep her in order and it would be all right. Perhaps he did keep her in order during his lifetime. But it was not good for Jehoram to have her as wife. I think he was bad enough himself, but she made him worse.

At last, after a good and long life, the old King Jehosaphat died. He had made his country great and prosperous, he had tried to make it religious, and now "he slept with his fathers and was buried with his fathers in the city of David, and Jehoram his son reigned in his stead."

§ 3. Queen Athaliah

Jehoram was king. Ah, yes, but Athaliah, the daughter of Jezebel, was queen. And like her mother she was a stronger character than her husband, for we are told "he walked in the way of the house of Ahab for he had the daughter of Ahab to wife: he did that which was evil in the sight of the Lord." (2 Kings viii. 18).

I suppose Queen Athaliah frequently visited her mother and corresponded with her. Cannot you imagine her excitement when the king's posts brought the news of that great day of Elijah on Mount Carmel and the story of Naboth's vineyard. Later on these posts brought her very awful news—of her father bleeding to death in his war chariot, of her brothers massacred by King Jehu in Samaria, and then, most awful of all, the news that told of the dead Jezebel, trampled to death under Jehu's horses, killed by Jehu. But these horrors did not make her repent. It seemed like as if the evil spirit of her dead mother had entered into the Queen of Judah. She was a very wicked woman. Her husband was bad enough himself. He killed his six brothers so that none of them could be king. He fostered and helped the false worship in the land. If his father knew in the Unseen Land (and I think he did, I think they always know about our life here), he must have been very sorry for that horrible mistake of his life in bringing Athaliah to Judah.

I don't think Jehoram was very happy in his home or in his kingdom. Wickedness does not bring a man much comfort as he grows older. He knew well that God was displeased with him. One day he knew it better when some messenger from the northern mountains brought him a letter—from whom, do you think? No less a person than the great Elijah himself. I daresay he had been observing Athaliah's life since she left her father's palace. Now he sends a letter, a written prophecy to her husband, which, I think, frightened pretty well both the husband and wife. They knew enough of Elijah to be afraid when he pronounced God's judgments on evil-doing. The letter said that God was angry with him for his great wickedness in killing his brothers and misleading his people, and that punishment would fall upon his family, and that he himself should die of a horrible disease. All of which came to pass.

§ 4. A Romantic Story

Surely no wonder if God's patience grew exhausted with these wicked kings and people, the nation that He had chosen out of all the world to help the rest of the world towards Him. After Jehoram's death came his son Ahaziah. Of him we are told, "He walked in the ways of the house of Ahab, for his mother was his counsellor to do wickedly." (2 Chronicles xxii. 3). What an awful thing to be said of a mother.

But there is much worse to be said of her. Before her son had been king for a year he was murdered by Jehu in Samaria, and immediately when the wicked old queen heard it she killed her son's young children— killed all the seed royal, all the descendants of David who might lay claim to the throne, and she made herself queen upon the throne of Judah. What a nice sort of queen to have over the people of the Lord! One often wonders at God's patience with wicked rulers whose example is injuring His people. They must surely be worse than wicked private people.

*   *   *   *   *   *   *   *

And now comes a most romantic episode in the history. Six years have elapsed since Queen Athaliah seized the crown. They have been six years of idolatry and wickedness. The people hate the queen, but they are afraid of her, and she feels herself quite secure, as there is no possible heir to the throne left alive. Ah! she does not know what a mine is under her. She does not see the little secret meetings at the house of Jehoiada, the high priest; she does not see the little boy of seven years old whom the priests and Levites and nobles and captains of the army are so much interested in at every meeting; she does not dream that at that slaughter of little princes six years ago one little infant boy was snatched away and hidden by the wife of the high priest.

But so it was. Jehoiada, the high priest, had married into the royal family. His wife, Jehosheba, on the night of the massacre, managed to snatch off her infant nephew and hide him with his nurse in the "storeroom of the mattresses" in the palace. By-and-by she and her husband brought the little Joash to one of the chambers of the Temple, and after a little while nobody suspected who he was except the few who were in the secret. Jehoiada had to move very cautiously. He whispered the secret to one and another whom he could trust, and as the queen grew more unpopular the friends of the little prince grew bolder. They whispered to the soldiers, to some of the nobles, to the priests, that a prince of the House of David was alive. It was a delightful and exciting surprise. They had thought that God's promise had failed and that the House of David was extinct. Now they were full of eagerness and enthusiasm. They would die for their little prince if it were needed.

§ 5. God Save the King!

We draw near the end.

Sabbath morning in Jerusalem. The crowds are preparing to go to church. They little know what an exciting church service is before them. All night Jehoiada has been making his arrangements. Four bands of the king's bodyguard are to be quietly behind the Temple gates. Two more bands are to stand to the right and left of a new platform erected before the altar. Arms are distributed secretly amongst the rest of the soldiers.

Now the Temple courts are crowded with worshippers strangely excited and expecting they know not what. Wondering they see the high priest stand forth to tell the story of the young prince's rescue, and in the midst of the excitement he brings forth the little boy between the rows of armed men. The crowd watch, wild with excitement, as the child stands on the high platform and the crown is placed upon his head and a copy of the Scriptures placed upon the crown. Then the anointing oil is placed upon his head, the trumpets ring out the royal salute, and the crowd can keep quiet no longer. From every voice, priest and noble and soldier and worshipper, goes up one great and repeated cry, "God save the King! God save the King!" It was the shout of relief from dread, of hatred to the queen, of wild joy that they had a king of David's house again. Perhaps with some it was a shout, too, of thankfulness to God. It was many a day since such joyous uproar had been heard in the Temple.

Suddenly, in the midst of the tumult, there is a startled hush. The great door flies open. The queen is coming in to know the meaning of it all. Silently, half-frightened, they watch her as she passes angrily up the Temple. Then she sees it all. "Treason! treason!" she cries, and turns rapidly to go. They let her go, but armed men followed her, and as she reached the doors of her palace the swords were out and in a moment she lay dead on the palace steps. Like the fate of her mother, Jezebel, twenty years ago! Don't you think it is hardly worth being wicked at such a price as that, even if there were no God to care? Ah! the devil is a bad paymaster.

(Read 1 Kings xv. 9 etc.; 2 Kings xi.)

QUESTIONS FOR LESSON XVI

Now remind yourselves about the nation being split into two kingdoms. What were their names? What King split the nation into two?

Which of the two have we been reading of up to this?

What happened to it?

Now we read about the other. What was it called? Was it northern or southern?

What did King Asa do for religion?

What bad mistake was in King Jehosaphat's marriage?

Who was his wife? Who was her mother?

By what crime did she make herself queen?

Now tell briefly the romantic story of this Queen Athaliah and the little prince Joash.

THE KINGS OF THE GREAT PROPHETS

2 Kings XI., parts of 2 Chronicles XXV., XXVI.

Thus the boy King Joash came to the throne, much as the boy king Edward VI. long ago in England. And, like him, this boy's heart was set on right. And like him, too, this boy king in Judah was too much under the rule of his elders. Let that pass for the present. Do you remember already, in the coronations of Saul and David and Solomon and Rehoboam, what a grand start in life God gave each of them. And each of them in some degree disappointed God. I don't think that any one of them had a more hopeful start in life than this young King Joash. It is a delightfully refreshing story after all the horror and misery and sin of the wicked rulers and people before.

§ 1. Jehoiada's Crusade

That story of the Sabbath Coronation is not over yet.

Jehoiada, the high priest, saw how deeply the people were moved at the coronation of the young king. So he gathered them all around him into a solemn assembly. No doubt he reminded them of all God's goodness to the nation from the beginning, and of the shameful way they had been treating Him, and how, in spite of it all, God had now delivered them from the wicked rule of Athaliah and given them a king of the House of David again. I am only guessing what he said. But the conclusion of the assembly is told in the Bible, "Jehoiada made a covenant between the Lord and the king and the people, that they should be the Lord's people." (2 Kings xi. 17). Is not that very beautiful after all the black wickedness of the past! God's Holy Spirit was surely stirring strongly in them just then. There are times in the life of every man and woman and boy and girl and nation when there seems a special rush of high and good desires, a sort of high-water mark of good. Perhaps on Confirmation Day, or at First Communion, or after a talk with one's mother, I think these are the special visions of God to show all that He intends and hopes for us. That Sabbath was a high-water mark of good to the men of Judah. And it kept them higher for many years.

As they were leaving the Temple again the priest spoke to them, this time more sternly and fiercely. Like Peter the Hermit in Europe long ago, he was calling them to a crusade against the filthy idolatry that had so cursed them. Soon the fierce excitement arose, "We will smash down the idol house." And out of the Temple they rushed, as crowds will rush, with the fierce delight of smashing up things. I think crowds are like mischievous boys. They love smashing things. I think it was partly righteous zeal for the Lord and partly hatred of idols, but partly, too, the delight of breaking down the idol house. "They broke it thoroughly in pieces," we are told, "and slew Mattan, the Baal priest, before his altars." (2 Kings xi. 18).

Then they returned and marched from the Temple to the palace with the soldiers in front and all the people, and they brought the little king in grand joyous procession and placed him on the throne of Judah. "So," it says, "all the people rejoiced and the city was quiet." Full time it should be. For surely never in the history of the city had there been such an exciting Sabbath day.

§ 2. Men Who Cannot Stand Alone

Such was young King Joash's fair start in life. And for a time he seemed to live up to it. As he grew older he became very desirous to repair the Temple of Solomon. You see, he had been brought up in the Temple, like young Samuel of old, with the children of the high priest, and so he knew more about it and cared more about it. It needed repairing and restoring very badly indeed. Since the day when Rehoboam gave away the golden shields it had been repeatedly ransacked for treasures to buy off invaders. Then Queen Athaliah had taken the very stones of its walls to build her idol temple. So it was a long task. For years and years this pious young king worked at it, and his people willingly gave the money, and Jehoiada, the high priest, directed it all.

I am afraid Jehoiada directed Joash too much. He was a good holy old man, and his influence was all for good, but after the king had grown to manhood I think it would have been better for him to stand more on his own feet and decide things for himself. I do not like men that lean too much for guidance, even on good men. It weakens them. At any rate, it looks like it here. Jehoiada lived a very long life, loved and honoured by the king and people. When he died they paid him the highest honour of burying him in the royal sepulchres, and Zacharias, his son, became the new high priest. I daresay he and the young king had been children together in the old days in the Temple.

But somehow, after the old priest died, there came a change in King Joash. He had no longer his old friend to lean on; so, being a weak man, he turned to some of the nobles and aristocracy in the city. Judging from the prophet's accounts this aristocracy of Jerusalem was a very poor set, something like those in Paris before the French Revolution. They wanted the idol worship back with all its grand ceremonies and all its abominable sins. Suddenly the prophets and religious people were startled to hear that the King had actually given permission. To many of his people it was a great surprise. To many of you, perhaps, too. Not to us older people who have watched the lives of men like Joash, men who, under the influence of a strong friend, or because of the opinion of the company in which they live, have kept right, and thought themselves right. You can't be sure of any man till you see what he will do when left quite alone. I'm afraid some weak people who seem good like Joash, because they are led by others, might find out sad things about themselves if they knew all. It is a good prayer, "Search me, O God, and know my heart, try me and know my thoughts, and see if there be any way of wickedness in me, and lead me in the way everlasting."

§ 3. "The Blood of Zacharias"

Soon the old wicked days began to come back. Then came indignant protests from the prophets (2 Chronicles xxiv. 27). But all of no avail. King Joash went on in his evil, though I am sure his conscience was vexing him.

And then came the worst deed of his life. There was one man who felt all this very terribly, the new high priest Zacharias. He was the son of the old high priest Jehoiada, and had probably grown up as a child with Joash in the Temple chambers. I daresay he spoke plainly to the king in memory of their old days, and of the dear old high priest, his father, who had taught them both about God. If so it was no use. Then Zacharias could bear it no longer, and one day in the Temple, as he stood on high above the people, the Spirit of God came upon him, and he sternly rebuked the king and the people, and ended with the warning, "Because ye have forsaken the Lord He hath also forsaken you."

Perhaps Joash was at church that day, but if not someone told him, and he was very angry. How dare the priest rebuke him in public before the people! Do you remember the story in English history when Henry II. uttered the impatient words about Thomas à Becket,

178

"Will no one rid me of this proud priest?" and how the fierce Norman knights set out and murdered à Becket before the altar, though probably the king had not really desired this at all. Perhaps this was all that King Joash did. One hopes it, because of the memory of the dead Jehoiada. But the story says worse than this, that they conspired against Zacharias and stoned him with stones *at the commandment of the king* in the court of the Lord's house. Thus Joash the king remembered not the kindness which Jehoiada his father showed him, but slew his son. And when he died he said, "The Lord look on it and requite it!" (2 Chronicles xxiv. 20-23).

The cruel deed was long remembered in Jerusalem. Indeed, the Jewish commentators on the Bible say that the blood of the dead priest, like the blood of Rizzio in Holyrood Palace in Edinburgh, could not be washed out. It was reported that long afterwards, when the Babylonian General entered the Temple at the time of the Captivity, the blood stain still bubbled up before him. Do you remember how sternly our Lord refers to it (Matthew xxiii. 35), "from the blood of righteous Abel to the blood of Zacharias, the son of Barachias, who was slain between the temple and the altar." You see this book of 2 Chronicles was the last book in the old Jewish Bible, so that the reference is to the first murder and the last murder recorded in the Scriptures.

How miserable it all is when we had begun to hope for Judah! How sorrowful to think of the closing days of this king to whom God had given such great advantages! At the end of the year he was defeated shamefully by the Syrians, and as he lay sick after the battle his own servants murdered him in his bed. What a number of disappointing people God has to bear with. Do not you wonder what He does with them when they die and go back to Him with all their miserable disappointing life? That will be one of the great revelations to us at the other side of the grave. Oh, the patience of the Father with us all!

§ 4. Prophets and Kings

After Joash comes a succession of four kings— Amaziah, Uzziah, Jotham and Ahaz, of whom there is not much to say except about the excessive wickedness of the last. The chief interest of their reigns is the fact that the greatest prophets of the world lived then. The prophets are the men who can see God's eternal Law of Righteousness always, and see that nothing else in the whole world is worth comparing with it. Therefore, it will often happen in the world's history that prophets are much more important people than kings, because righteousness is much more important than power. I daresay that some of these kings thought themselves very important, but their very names are almost forgotten. I daresay some of these prophets of God thought themselves of no consequence at all, and wondered that God should help them to see or say anything helpful to the nation, but some of their names will never be forgotten while the world lasts.

Now keep in mind the names of these four kings and then turn up some of the separate books of the prophecies in your Bible and read the following verses:—

Amos i. 1.— "The words of Amos, who was among the herdmen of Tekoa, in the days of Uzziah, king of Judah, and Jeroboam, king of Israel, two years before the earthquake."

Micah i. 1.—"The word of the Lord that came to Micah, the Morasthite, in the days of Jotham, Ahaz, and Hezekiah, kings of Judah."

Isaiah i. 1.—"The vision of Isaiah, the son of Amos, which he saw concerning Judah and Jerusalem, in the days of Uzziah, Jotham, Ahaz, and Hezekiah, kings of Judah."

People seldom read these wonderful prophecies, because by themselves they are so hard to understand. People take little interest in the histories of these insignificant kings, because they seem unimportant, and one knows so little about them. But you see at once how much more interesting would be the histories and prophecies if we got the habit of connecting them together—if, for example, before reading the books of Micah or Isaiah we should first read the histories of their kings, in the books of Kings and Chronicles, or if, when reading the histories of these kings, we should find out what these prophets, who lived and knew them, thought about them and their people. In the next chapter we shall try briefly to do this in some degree.

(Read 2 Kings xi., parts of 2 Chronicles xxv., xxvi., and the references above.)

QUESTIONS FOR LESSON XVII

Who were (1) Jehoiada, (2) Joash, (3) Zacharias?

Did young King Joash get a good start in life? Who was his guide and friend?

Did he keep on well? Tell some of his bad deeds.

A good start from God; a bad ending—who was to blame?

In this he was like an earlier king. Whom?

What lesson do we get from their lives?

What do you know of (1) Amos, (2) Micah, (3) Isaiah?

Tell me again how people should read the books of the Prophets.

ISAIAH, THE ROYAL PROPHET OF JERUSALEM

2 Chronicles XXVI., Isaiah VI.

§ 1. Forthtelling

The last chapter closed with mention of the four kings after Joash—Amaziah, Uzziah, Jotham, Ahaz. Nothing very important is told of them in the history, and their importance for us lies in the fact that the greatest prophets of the world lived and preached in their reigns. Do you notice that I say "preached"? This is because I want you to understand that the chief work of the prophets was preaching, not prophesying, about the future. They did on the whole very little of that. As we read their prophecies we find they are chiefly insisting on the great eternal law of God that Right is Right and must always be done, that Wrong is Wrong and must never be done. No matter what dangers may be risked by doing right, no matter what gains may be won by doing wrong. That is the law of God, which is eternal.

It must be true always and everywhere in the furthest ages, in the most distant planets. There can never be a change in that Eternal Law. Will you learn off by heart this sentence, "The chief work of the prophets was not *fore*telling but *forth*telling," i.e. telling forth the eternal law of God, and showing how it applied in their own day. Sometimes they prophesied about future things. Sometimes it was shown them that certain great events would happen, or that punishment would follow certain sins. Sometimes, too, most wonderful of all, there came to them from God very beautiful vague beliefs in some great Being that should come in the future who should be the great Comforter and Leader and King of men, and who should somehow be like God Himself. I don't think they themselves understood half what they saw or guessed about the coming of our Lord to earth. They often got it mixed up with other things. Yet, in the midst of the worst threatenings, they were continually looking forward to some "golden age" for the people in the far future when God should be very close to men. And these prophecies must have had a great deal to do with the general feeling of expectation of some Messiah at the time of our Lord's birth. Yet, none the less, be it clearly remembered, that the prophet's chief duty was not *fore*telling future events, but rather *forth*telling present duties.

§ 2. The Leper King

Amaziah's reign is not of much interest. He was murdered by conspirators like many kings of his time.

Then we are told *"all the people"* took Uzziah his son, who was sixteen years old, and made him king. I suppose that means that "all the people" liked this young prince. He had a very long reign of 52 years, a splendid prosperous reign. He did well for the country. He strengthened Jerusalem. He increased the army. He increased the trade. But there were some serious troubles, which are interesting to us, chiefly because of the impression they made on some of the prophets.

One day, after a very hot summer, when the land was parched with drought, suddenly the light grew dim as if thunder were coming, and over the hill tops came masses of dark cloud and dense masses of locusts, which devoured every blade of grass and left the land in desolation. Later on, on a terrible day in the king's life, the whole city rocked with a violent earthquake, cleaving the mountains and valleys asunder. Josephus, the Jewish historian, says that it rent asunder the Temple roof, and that the king, standing at the altar within, was stricken with leprosy at that moment. At any rate, the leprosy was a fact. For some act of presumption in the Temple we are told the old king was struck with leprosy, and they had to keep him in a lonely leper house till he died (2 Chronicles xxvi. 21). A very sad fate for such a great, prosperous king. Perhaps, though, it was only God's kind way of taking him "aside from the multitude," as our Lord long afterwards took a poor man for his good. I should not wonder if the poor old lonely leper king grieved and prayed about the wickedness of the nation more than he had ever done before.

§ 3. Joel, Amos, Micah

For, indeed, with all its outward prosperity, Judah, in the time of these four kings, was in a very bad state, as we shall learn from their great prophet preachers later on. Idolatry was rife, with its evil abominable customs. The men of the higher classes were much given to drunkenness. The women were vain and dressy, and of very evil life.

And the worst of it was that they had got into quite a comfortable way of mixing up their sin and their religion. They thought that if they went to church at the proper time it was all right. "So many fasts, so many festivals, so many sacrifices," they said, "what has the Lord to complain of?" It is a curious attitude that sometimes comes to people substituting forms and services for one supreme thing in God's sight, Righteousness, Right doing.

I suppose that was especially the reason why so many prophets arose just then. You see the prophet was the man who was most deeply inspired to see that Right and Duty and Character were the supreme things—that all churchgoing and ceremonies were only for the sake of these. "What doth the Lord require of thee," cried one of these preachers, "but to do justly, and to love mercy, and to walk humbly with thy God." (Micah vi.).

There were two men who were watching the locust plague and the earthquake. The name of the one was Joel, a stern preacher of judgment. You can picture him in his hair cloth robe preaching through the streets of Jerusalem warning King Uzziah's people of the plague of locusts that should come like a solid army over the land.

"The land is as the garden of Eden before them, and behind them a desolate wilderness. Their appearance is as the appearance of horses; and as horsemen, so do they run. At their appearance the people are in anguish, all faces wax pale. They run like mighty men; they climb like men of war; they break not their ranks," etc. (Joel ii.)

And he ends with that penitential sentence so familiar to us all, "Rend your heart and not your garments and turn to the Lord your God, for He is gracious and merciful, slow to anger and of great kindness, and repenteth Him of the evil." Read the whole of the 2nd chapter of Joel as a series of short sermons for the times.

And another man was watching also—a shepherd like David, and a gatherer of coarse figs. His name was Amos. We have read of him before in the history of the northern Israel, for he felt called to leave his lonely country life in Judah, and to go away to Samaria to preach about God in the wicked court of Jeroboam II. I don't think he did much good there, for the court chaplain, the priest of Bethel, turned him out of the king's chapel and told him to go home and mind his own people (Amos vii. 12, 13). But when you read the sermons of Amos remember that he was one of the subjects of "the leper king." He says he was called by God "in the days of Uzziah, King of Judah, and Jeroboam, King of Israel, two years before the earthquake." (Amos i.).

And another prophet, Micah, the Morasthite, came just a little later and tells of all the evils of the land under Uzziah's son and grandson. See his first chapter: "The word of the Lord that came to Micah in the days of Jotham, Ahaz, and Hezekiah." I daresay these kings knew well his prophecy, which long afterwards was quoted to the wise men from the East seeking the child Jesus, "And thou Bethlehem, in the land of Judah, art not the least among the princes of Judah: for out of thee shall come a Governor, that shall rule my people Israel." (Matthew ii. 6). Probably one of them was present when his great sermon was preached about Balaam and Balak, "What doth the Lord require of thee, but to do justly, and love mercy, and walk humbly with thy God." (Micah vi.).

§ 4. Isaiah's Call

All these were great prophets, but they were as nothing to their famous leader, the greatest of all the prophets of that time. He was called of God in a very sorrowful time. The leper King Uzziah was shut away in his leper house old and dying, and wickedness was spreading in the land, and it seemed as if God had gone away and forgotten His people.

One day, at this sorrowful time, a godly young noble,[1] Isaiah, the son of Amos, a cousin of the king, went into the Temple, I suppose to think and pray over the troubles of the land, and to wonder, perhaps, like many another, why God did not do more to help. He little knew how much God was going to do that day to help not Judah only, but all the world since!

[1] Jewish tradition says he was a cousin of the king.

The young man was perhaps gazing upon the altar and the fire and the incense rising in a great cloud of smoke filling the house, when suddenly all that he saw became glorified into a vision. It is the only vision of his life—at least, the only one that he mentions, but it was enough to alter his whole life and call him to be amongst the greatest of the prophets of God.

Long afterwards he tells the story himself:—

"In the year that King Uzziah died I saw also the Lord sitting upon a throne, high and lifted up, and his train filled the temple.

Above it stood the seraphim: each had six wings; with twain he covered his face, and with twain he covered his feet, and with twain he did fly.

And one cried unto another, and said, Holy, holy, holy, is the Lord of hosts: the whole earth is full of his glory.

And the posts of the door moved at the voice of him that cried, and the house was filled with smoke.

Then said I, Woe is me! for I am undone; because I am a man of unclean lips: for mine eyes have seen the King, the Lord of hosts.

Then flew one of the seraphim unto me, having a live coal in his hand, which he had taken with the tongs from off the altar;

And he laid it upon my mouth, and said, Lo, this hath touched thy lips; and thine iniquity is taken away, and thy sin purged.

Also I heard the voice of the Lord, saying, Whom shall I send, and who will go for us? Then said I, Here am I; send me."

A grand commission surely to receive from God. But surely, too, a very sad commission. For he is told, v. 10, what the result of his message is going to be. The people of Judah are so attached to wrong that they do not want to see the right, and his message will—

"make their ears heavy and shut their eyes, lest they see with their eyes, and hear with their ears, and understand with their heart, and be healed." Then said I, "Lord, how long?" And he answered, "Until cities be waste without inhabitant, and houses without man, and the land become utterly waste, and the Lord have removed men far away," etc. (Isaiah vi.).

§ 5. Isaiah and King Ahaz

I wonder what Isaiah thought about it all? Did he see that it meant that he should go on teaching and teaching in vain until at last the Captivity came and the whole nation should be swept away to learn in sorrowful exile what they would not learn in those prosperous days.

At any rate, when at the end of his life he looked on this vision, he must have seen that it meant something like this. He says no more about his vision. He does not tell with what feelings he returned home that day, and if he passed the house of the old leper king. We never hear another word about this vision. But when you open your Bible and see the big book of Isaiah's sermons and prophecies you will remember how they began. I am afraid they are not all in their right order in the book. You see they were quite separate utterances; and I do not suppose that Isaiah had any hand in the final arranging of them. Probably they were not collected or edited until long after his death. You know if some one tried to arrange a clergyman's pile of sermons after his death they would find it hard to put them in the right order. So with Isaiah and with Jeremiah after him. Indeed, a most interesting study is first to learn the history of the time carefully, and then to try and guess out in what order of time Isaiah or Jeremiah preached these sermons.

For example, the very first chapter seems at first to refer to the close of old King Uzziah's reign; but as we read on we see it cannot, because Uzziah's was a prosperous reign, and this first chapter tells of "your country desolate and your cities burned with fire." (*ch.* i. 7).

We guess from that the period he refers to. The old leper king died very soon after Isaiah's call. After him his son Jotham reigned for some years, a fairly good man, and then came his son Ahaz, one of the worst and most mischievous of all the Kings of Judah. And "the Lord brought Judah low because of Ahaz who trespassed sore against the Lord." (2 Chronicles xxviii. 19). The Kings of Israel and Syria first attacked him, but Isaiah was sent to tell him that God would deliver him, and He did. But Ahaz was no better. Then the Edomites and the Philistines attacked him fiercely and seized several towns and kept them, and wrought desolation through the whole country. This is evidently the time of this prophecy of Isaiah in his first chapter, which gives you some notion of the sort of king and people and the state of society that the prophet had to deal with and that God had to put up with. The chapter tells of their wickedness and the misery of the land, and how they thought that their sacrifices and church services without any real effort after righteousness would satisfy the Holy God. Read Isaiah i.:—

"Hear, O heavens, and give ear, O earth, for the Lord hath spoken, I have nourished and brought up children, and they have rebelled against me, The ox knoweth his owner, and the ass his master's crib: but Israel doth not know, my people do not consider. Ah, sinful nation, a people laden with iniquity, a seed of evildoers, children that have dealt corruptly. . . . .

Why will ye be stricken any more, that ye revolt more and more? The whole head is sick, and the whole heart faint. Your country is desolate, your cities are burned with fire, your land, strangers devour it in your presence, and it is desolate, as overthrown by strangers. . . . .

To what purpose is the multitude of your sacrifices unto me? saith the Lord. I am full of burnt offerings. . . . . I delight not in the blood of bullocks and lambs. . . . Bring no more vain oblations. Your new moons and your appointed feasts my soul hateth. . . . . Wash you, make you clean, put away the evil of your doings from before my eyes. Cease to do evil, learn to do well. . . . .

Come now, and let us reason together, saith the Lord: though your sins be as scarlet, they shall be white as snow, and though they be red like crimson, they shall be as wool."

Should not you expect now that Ahaz and his people would turn to the Lord for help? Not a bit of it. He turned to the great cruel King of Assyria and gave him all his treasures and made himself a subject king to this great enemy of Israel.

Thus he got peace with dishonour. And with peace he grew worse and worse. He "walked according to the abominations of the heathen." He sacrificed his own son to the brutal Moloch. He sacrificed and burnt incense on the high places, on the hills, and under every green tree." (2 Kings xvi. 3, 4). The whole society of Jerusalem was bad. The princes were rebellious and companions of thieves; the judges gave false judgment following after reward. "Men rose early in the morning to follow strong drink and continued till night till the wine inflamed them." (Isaiah *v.* 11). The women were as bad, "they walk with stretched forth necks and wanton eyes, and their anklets and crescents and bracelets and rings and nose jewels." (Isaiah iii.).

It seemed as if Isaiah could do nothing, as if the long-suffering, patient God could do nothing but let them drift on to the great crisis of their fate—the Captivity. Just what God had revealed to Isaiah when He called him. Yet in spite of it all God had good designs for them in the future.

(Read 2 Chronicles xxvi., Isaiah vi. and references as above to other prophets.)

QUESTIONS FOR LESSON XVIII

What did we mean by saying that the prophets did more forthtelling than foretelling?

We have here three lesser prophets and one very great prophet. Name them.

Who was the "leper king"?

Tell the story of Isaiah's call to be a prophet.

Who tells the story? Where?

Had he a happy or a sad time? Why?

LESSON XIX

HEZEKIAH AND THE REFORMATION

2 Kings XVIII. 1-6 and parts of

2 Chronicles XXIX., XXX.

§ 1. Who Influenced Hezekiah?

At last the wicked King Ahaz died, and it was a great relief to the land. Then his son Hezekiah came to the throne, a young man of twenty-five.

We have had a very ugly, discouraging history of Judah up to this. Now we are to have a change. For Hezekiah was not only a clever king, a wise ruler, a brave soldier, a skilful builder and engineer,[1] but also he was heart and soul devoted to God and righteousness. With such a father as King Ahaz one wonders at this. But I have already advised you in the story of the kings to watch out for their mothers. We read that Hezekiah's

---

[1] In next chapter I have to tell you of one of his engineering feats which was discovered for us a few years ago by a set of boys playing in Jerusalem.

194

mother was the daughter of Zechariah (2 Chronicles xxix. 1), and we have already seen that Zechariah, a prophet, had helped King Uzziah to be a good man (2 Chronicles xxvi. 5). Ah! it is the mothers that matter most. God does more by the holy mothers than by any other means. I believe this boy must have been much influenced by his mother.

Of course he would be influenced also by his famous relative Isaiah, who must have taught him a great deal about God. They were great friends these two, in spite of the disparity of years, and they were just the sort of influential men to work together to carry out a great reformation in the land.

I have only just found out that the prophet Micah, the rough, shaggy country prophet, had also his share in influencing Hezekiah. You remember Micah the Morasthite, who preached the two famous sermons, one about "thou Bethlehem in the land of Judah art not the least among the princes of Judah, for out of thee shall come a Governor that shall rule my people Israel," and the other in which the grand passage occurs, "What doth the Lord require of thee but to do justly, and to love mercy, and to walk humbly with thy God." It was probably in the beginning of Hezekiah's reign when much of the wicked results of his father's reign remained. The history says nothing of Micah's influence, but it comes out in a curious way some hundred years after. Look at Jeremiah xxvi. 18, 19, where an elder is pleading for Jeremiah when he was in danger of his life for speaking out disagreeable reproofs. He tells that once in earlier days Micah the Morasthite had stood

195

up before Hezekiah and his people and spoken stern, faithful words to the king and people. "Did Hezekiah and the men of Judah put him to death for it?" he asks. "Did Hezekiah not fear the Lord and entreat the favour of the Lord, and the Lord repented Him of the evil?" But for this generous pleading we should never have learned that Micah had anything to do with Hezekiah's great reformation.

§ 2. The Great Reformation

At any rate, whatever influenced him, the young king in his very first year set about this GREAT REFORMATION, and you may be sure Isaiah was heartily with him. Most kings in his case would have thought that this could wait. He had much else to do. He was in the humiliating position through his father's act of being subject to the King of Assyria, and he might well have tried to win freedom first. But I am sure Isaiah taught him that to get close to God and to do God's will was much more important to begin with.

He began by cleansing the defiled and disused Temple, and refitting it and preparing it for decent, reverent worship again. For sixteen days they worked at it till the altar and the shewbread table and all the sacred vessels which King Ahaz had cast away were prepared and sanctified. Then came the opening service, very beautiful and touching, and strange though it seems after the wicked days of the last reign, the people seemed quite on his side. I think that is so encouraging for poor humanity. Even bad, careless men have enough of the nature made in the image of God to be touched by good deeds even if they do not do them.

Then a happy thought came to the king. "Could not we celebrate the reopening of the Temple by a great national revival of the Passover Feast?" The Passover seems to have been neglected for centuries. We hear nothing of it ever since the days of Joshua. This is very puzzling. At any rate, Hezekiah resolved that it should be restored, and as he thought of it there came to him the earnest desire that if it were possible, not only his own kingdom of Judah but the great Northern Kingdom of Israel also should take part. Surely a mad, hopeless scheme it seemed. The two kingdoms had been separated and hostile since the days of Solomon, eight hundred years ago. The Northern Kingdom, too, had something else than Passovers to think of just then, for the terrible Assyrians were threatening its borders, and its people were within a few years of being swept away into captivity for ever. Nothing makes me think so highly of Hezekiah as the fact that he should have the courage and enthusiasm to attempt such a hopeless project. I like the people that attempt impossible things, that are not afraid of making mistakes. The cold, cautious people that do not ever make mistakes usually do not ever make anything else either.

§ 3. The Northern Post

The king wrote such a beautiful touching letter to the whole nation. It begins, "Ye children of Israel, turn again to the Lord," and it ends "for the Lord your God is gracious and merciful, and will not turn away His face from you." (2 Chronicles xxx.). "So," we are told, "the posts passed from city to city through the country of Ephraim and Manasseh; but they laughed them to scorn, and mocked them." Just what we might expect. Probably Hezekiah's advisers were pleased to tell him, "We told you so!" But the Bible says:

"Nevertheless divers of Asher and Manasseh and of Zebulum humbled themselves, and came to Jerusalem. Also in Judah was the hand of God to give them one heart to do the commandment of the king and princes, by the word of the Lord." (2 Chronicles xxx. 10-12).

So you see, the efforts of Hezekiah were not so foolish as they looked. As you see, too, the earnest preaching of Isaiah and Micah had not been all in vain in Judah, and all the pleading of Amos and Hosea, and the rest of God's teachers, had not been in vain either in that poor miserable kingdom of the North Israel just going away into its captivity.

It was a wonderful time that Passover week in Jerusalem. It seems to have stirred the nation to its depths. "There was great joy in Jerusalem," we are told, "for since the time of Solomon, the son of David, King of Israel, there was not the like in Jerusalem." I like the statement that Hezekiah encouraged the great congregation, and that the priests and the Levites arose and blessed the people; and I like especially to read of the poor stupid Northern people who in their ignorance had come to the Passover without going through the ceremony of purification as commanded by Moses. This was reckoned a very serious thing. And many a stern holy Jew would have forbidden them to come. But Hezekiah prayed for them, saying: "The good Lord pardon every one that setteth his heart to seek the God of his fathers, even though he be not cleansed with the purification of the sanctuary." I like that. I read once of a poor idiot that was forbidden to come to the Holy Communion because he did not understand about the Lord Jesus clearly, "I don't understand about Him," he said; "but I would die for Him."

How pleased the king must have been, and how pleased Isaiah and Micah must have been. Aye, and don't you think the Lord was pleased, too, to see this wonderful stirring of religious life after all these years of wrong?

The people seem to have gone half wild with excitement and delight. Off they set in crowds in a great crusade through the land, not only through Judah, but through Israel in the North, breaking in pieces the pillars and the Asherim, and breaking down the high places and the altars of the idols. The poor king of the Northern Kingdom could not oppose them. He was in hand grips with his great enemy, the King of Assyria, and could attend to nothing else. I daresay they did some fierce and foolish things in that wild raid of theirs, but one might forgive much in that great zeal for God after the long years of sin.

I think it must have been just then that the king in his zeal did a very brave thing. A right thing and a wise thing it was, but I should fancy a very unpopular thing. You remember the great Brazen Serpent of Moses' days

(Numbers xxi. 8, 9). It had been preserved with deep reverence for centuries as a holy memorial of God's dealings in the Wilderness, and at last in the idolatrous days, the people took to worshipping it. Hezekiah, therefore, resolved to break it in pieces. It was a daring act. It was all very well to break down false idols, but I do not think the people liked this breaking up a thing that was a sign memorial of God's presence. Even the nations around heard of it as an impious act against the Lord. In the next chapter we shall see how the Assyrians had heard of it as an irreligious act (2 Kings xviii. 22). I greatly admire the man who did this unpopular act, calmly and quietly regardless of consequences, just because it was right. That is the sort of man to work great reforms.

§ 4. The Making of the Bible

One wonders how much did Hezekiah do in the making of our Bible. When you are older there is a very interesting question before you. How did the Bible get made? Who collected the books? Why were some books put in and some left out? That is too long a question to talk about here. But you should know that in some wonderful way God's providence was, century by century, gradually forming a Jewish Bible by means of the Jewish Church. Moses' writings were being preserved and arranged and completed by the wise men of that Church. And the many records of God's dealings in the days of the Judges and of the Kings, many of them now lost, were being stored up, so that historians later on should write out those histories as we have them to-day. Then there were all sorts of odd scraps of prophecies and odd hymns and psalms that might easily get lost. Indeed, many of them did get lost and destroyed. The wonder is that any of them escaped in all those long years of neglect of religion.

You may be sure Hezekiah would think of this matter in his great reformation. We have only a few hints. Look at the ancient Jewish heading over Proverbs xxv., the beginning of a new collection: "These also are proverbs of Solomon which the men of Hezekiah King of Judah copied out." I wonder how much besides those "men of Hezekiah" did. Did they collect also the psalms, the Jewish hymn-books, which were probably knocking about in a bad state all over the Temple when he was cleansing it? On this day of the great Passover we read that "he set the Levites in the house of the Lord with cymbals, with psalteries, and with harps, according to the commandment of David." Moreover, he "commanded the Levites to sing praises unto the Lord with the words of David and Asaph the seer." (2 Chronicles xxix. 25-30). I can fancy him superintending the cleaning of the Temple and watching the Levites gather up all the poor, tossed and torn hymn-books and odd sheets of psalms. Probably many a Christian man owes the comfort of certain psalms to that careful search of Hezekiah in the Temple during those sixteen days.

(Read parts of 2 Kings xviii. 1-6, parts of 2 Chronicles xxix. and xxx.)

QUESTIONS FOR LESSON XIX

Now comes a great and good king. Name?

What great prophet helped him?

How did he begin his great Reformation?

Tell of his beautiful letter to the people.

What kindness did he do the poor Northerners who came to the Passover unprepared?

What did he do about the brazen serpent? Why?

What do you know of the history of this brazen serpent?

What did Hezekiah do towards the making of the Bible?

HEZEKIAH AND SENNACHERIB

2 Kings XVIII. 13 to end of Chapter XIX.

and part of 2 Chronicles XXXII.

§ 1. Introduction

Five years have elapsed since Hezekiah's great Passover, years of peace and happiness and prosperity to the kingdom of Judah. Hezekiah, we are told, "had exceeding much riches and honour, and he provided him treasuries for silver, and for gold, and for precious stones, and for spices, and for shields, and for all manner of goodly vessels; storehouses also for the increase of corn, and wine, and oil; and stalls for all manner of beasts and flocks in folds, for God had given him very much substance." (2 Chronicles xxxii. 27). So far as we can judge, from the history, Judah had grown very prosperous. So far as we can judge from Isaiah's sermons, the prosperity did not bring increase of righteousness. The people did not keep on being enthusiastic about religion. In spite of all Hezekiah's efforts many of the old abuses crept back.

At the close of the five years there came very sad news from Israel in the North. Sargon, the King of Assyria, was besieging Samaria, and the city was in sore straits. I don't know why Hezekiah did not go to help them. Perhaps the King of Assyria was altogether too powerful, or perhaps Isaiah had taught him that the troubles of Samaria were from the hand of God. At last, in the sixth year of Hezekiah, came the sorrowful news, "Samaria is fallen and the whole kingdom of the ten tribes has been swept away into captivity to Assyria." So this little kingdom of Judah was now the sole remainder of the chosen people of God.

Year after year Judah prospered. Year after year, at odd times, tidings came to them from the Assyrian land, whither the Northern captives had gone. One summer there came the news that Sargon, the King of Assyria, was dead, and that the prince royal, Sennacherib, was king in his stead. I do not suppose the men of Judah cared much about the news. Very soon they had reason to care.

§ 2. Sennacherib

The young king Sennacherib was a man of great power and ability. We have in recent years discovered many of the Assyrian inscriptions, and they are most interesting reading. The account of Sennacherib's huge palace in Nineveh and his many victories and all the glory of his kingdom reads like a romance. And he certainly was conceited enough about his greatness. Here is his title—his opinion of himself on one of his own inscriptions:—

> SENNACHERIB
>
> THE GREAT THE POWERFUL KING
>
> THE KING OF THE ASSYRIANS, OF THE FOUR NATIONS
>
> THE DILIGENT RULER, THE FAVOURITE OF THE GREAT GODS
>
> THE GUARDIAN OF LAW, THE OBSERVER OF FAITH
>
> THE NOBLE HERO, THE GREAT WARRIOR, THE FIRST OF KINGS
>
> THE PUNISHER OF UNBELIEVERS AND OF WICKED MEN.

Modesty was not one of Sennacherib's weaknesses. So powerful was he that the only enemy that he had any fear of was Egypt. Now Palestine lay straight on the way to Egypt, and therefore Jerusalem and the other towns would be important outposts for either Egypt or Assyria (see map). There were in Jerusalem two political parties with a decided difference of opinion as to which of the two great nations they should lean toward. The party of reform, led by Isaiah, were always against Egypt. The rival party, led perhaps by "Shebna the scribe," were in favour of Egypt and against Assyria. Sennacherib evidently had learned of these political parties, and as he swept in with his powerful army against Egypt it would seem that he kept in mind this dangerous attitude in Jerusalem. He met and overthrew Tirhakah, King of Egypt, and then he turned on Judea. Terrified, the people listened for the tidings of his march. They heard of him as he came, swollen with pride and power, destroying all before him. The cities of Judah could make no resistance. Jerusalem itself was in very great danger.

Just then, when all were awed before the mighty conqueror, I like to see how the prophet of God looked on him. "The conqueror," he says, "who thinks himself a little god on earth, is only a poor instrument in the hand of the Lord to punish Judah." Imagine Isaiah proclaiming this to the terrified Jews in the city as they watched for the enemy:—

> "Ho, Assyrian! the rod of mine anger, the staff in whose hand is mine indignation! I will send him against this profane nation to take the spoil, to tread them down. Howbeit he meaneth not so, neither doth his heart think so. For he saith, 'Are not my princes all of them kings? Have I not destroyed great nations? Shall I not, as I have done to Samaria and her idols, so do to Jerusalem and her idols?'
>
> "Wherefore it shall come to pass that when the Lord hath performed his whole work on Jerusalem I will punish the stout heart of the King of Assyria, and the glory of his high looks. For he saith, 'By the strength of my hand I have done it.' Shall the axe boast itself against him that heweth therewith, shall the saw magnify itself against him that shakest it?
>
> "Therefore thus saith the Lord of Hosts, O my people, be not afraid of the Assyrian, though he smite thee with the rod. For yet a little while and the indignation shall be accomplished, and then the Lord of Hosts shall stir up against him a scourge," etc. (Isaiah x.)

What a power it must be in any man's life to see God's hand thus behind all earthly enemies and troubles. Imagine the people listening to this message as they watch from the walls, as they strain their eyes for the first sight of the invader, and then hear the prophet in a moment burst forth again as he sees with his mind's eye the bloodstained approach of the conqueror:—

"He is come to Aiath, he is passed through Migron; at Mich-mash he layeth up his baggage: they are over the pass: they have lodged at Geba: Ramah is trembling: Gibeah has fled; Cry aloud with thy voice, O daughter of Gallim: hearken, O Laisha, O thou poor Anathoth! Madena is a fugitive: This very day he halteth at Nob: he shaketh his hand at the mount of the daughter of Zion, at the hill of Jerusalem." (Isaiah x.)

§ 3. Hezekiah's Submission

Day after day the people of Jerusalem watched. Day after day the stories came in of conquest and bloodshed, and ruin of cities. Hezekiah kept a brave heart as long as he could. He repaired the walls and cut off the water supply from the enemy, and strengthened the garrison and encouraged them to fight. Then he got frightened. I am sure he did not ask Isaiah's advice, but if you want to know what he did, here is Sennacherib's story (boastful as usual), from one of his own inscriptions found in Nineveh; and to the side is the Bible story:—

BECAUSE HEZEKIAH KING OF JUDAH WOULD NOT SUBMIT TO MY YOKE I CAME UP AGAINST HIM. BY THE FORCE OF MY ARMS AND THE MIGHT OF MY POWER I TOOK 46 OF HIS STRONG FENCED CITIES AND OF THE SMALLER TOWNS WITH THE BATTERING RAMS AND MINES AND MISSILES I CAPTURED A COUNTLESS NUMBER. I CARRIED OFF 200,150 CAPTIVES WITH CATTLE A COUNTLESS MULTITUDE. AND

Now in the fourteenth year of King Hezekiah did Sennacherib King of Assyria come up against the fenced cities of Judah and took them. And Hezekiah King of Judah sent to the king of Assyria saying I have offended, return unto

HEZEKIAH I SHUT UP IN JERUSALEM LIKE A BIRD IN A CAGE. . . . THEN UPON THIS HEZEKIAH FELL THE FEAR OF THE POWER OF MY ARMS AND HE SENT OUT TO ME THE CHIEFS AND ELDERS OF JERUSALEM WITH 30 TALENTS OF GOLD AND 800 TALENTS OF SILVER AND DIVERS TREASURES. ALL THESE THINGS WERE BROUGHT TO ME AT NINEVEH THE CITY OF MY DOMINION HEZEKIAH'S TOKEN OF SUBMISSION TO MY POWER.—*Inscription from Rawlinson II. 435, quoted in Stanley's Jewish Church.*

me: that which thou puttest on me I will bear. And the King of Assyria appointed 300 talents of silver and 30 talents of gold. And Hezekiah gave him all the silver that was found in the house of the Lord and in the king's house, etc.—2 Kings xviii. 13-16.

I feel sure that Isaiah was grieved and angry when he heard of the king's decision, and more so when he saw the people shouting on the housetops rejoicing at this shameful peace. Probably his 22nd chapter expresses his feelings: "What aileth thee that thou art gone up to the housetops?" etc. Read the chapter and notice the stern rebuke of "Shebna the scribe" at the close. I wonder was it Shebna who counselled the king to do this cowardly deed?

§ 4. Rab-shakeh's Challenge

The Bible account is now a little difficult to understand. "After this," we are told, Sennacherib sent his servants, the Rab-shakeh, etc., with an army to Jerusalem (2 Chronicles xxxii. 9; 2 Kings xviii. 13).

If Hezekiah had submitted and made friends, why this army?

Why? It is not quite clear. But, from the words of

Rab-shakeh (2 Kings xviii. 21) about the folly of trusting in Egypt, it would seem either that Hezekiah had sought help from Egypt, or else that Sennacherib pretended to think he had, in order to destroy Jerusalem, which was a dangerous obstacle to his plans. This latter seems to have been Isaiah's opinion, for he says (Isaiah xxxiii. 8) that Sennacherib had broken the covenant.

At any rate, we have a most vivid picture, the Assyrian soldiers before the city, and the walls crowded with the garrison, and with vast numbers of citizens watching and listening. There were three Assyrian officers, the Tartan, or general, the Rab-saris, or chief eunuch, and the Rab-shakeh, or chief cupbearer. The latter was the speaker. It was a sort of game of bluff. Sennacherib was busy warring at Lachish and Libnah, and he evidently thought that since he could not come himself with his full army he might send this band to try if he could bully Hezekiah, who had been so badly frightened last year. I think he had chosen his messenger well. This scurrilous, blasphemous heathen cupbearer was just the man to frighten a timid king and people if they could be frightened at all.

The Rab-shaketh was very clever too. He had found out that in the Reformation days there was some bad feeling against the king for smashing the Brazen Serpent and throwing down some of the altars in which some images representing Jehovah used to be worshipped. "Do you trust in Egypt?" he cries. "He is a broken reed. Do you say you trust in God? Why, Hezekiah has broken down His emblems. Do you trust in yourselves? Why, I will lend you 2,000 horses if you can even set a man on each of them." So the clever ambassador goes on till the Jewish officers get frightened for its effect on the people. "Speak to us in Syrian," they asked, "that the people may not hear. Don't speak in the Jew's language." "Nay," cried the Assyrian, "I am sent to speak to the people." And then comes the blasphemous appeal to the people. "Do not let Hezekiah deceive you, saying Jehovah will deliver us. Hath any of the gods of the nations ever delivered his land out of the hand of the King of Assyria? Where are the gods of Hamath and Arpad and Sepharvaim and Hena and Ivah? What god has ever delivered his country from us that Jehovah should be able to deliver Jerusalem out of my hand?"

"But all the people held their peace and answered not a word, as the king had commanded." So the Assyrian had to return with no reply to his master, and Hezekiah rent his clothes when they told him of the blasphemy, and sent for Isaiah to pray far the people.

When the Assyrian officers returned to their king to tell him that they had failed, he wrote to Hezekiah a letter even more blasphemous against God than were the words of his messenger: "Let not thy God in whom thou trustest deceive thee saying Jerusalem shall not be taken. Have the gods of the nations delivered them whom my father destroyed?" Poor stupid heathen king, who did not know he was only like a rod in the hands of God! Many people who read the newspapers to-day are just like him. They do not see God's hand behind everything, and therefore they get frightened at wars and catastrophes. They do not see that nothing matters except wrongdoing, for God is behind all. Isaiah did see.

God had taught him, and he tried to teach Hezekiah and his people.

§ 5. *The Great Deliverance*

So Hezekiah went off to the Temple and spread out the letter of Sennacherib before the Lord. And, I think, his prayer showed that he was learning Isaiah's lesson.

"O Lord the God of Israel, which dwellest between the cherubims, thou art the God, even thou alone, of all the kingdoms of the earth; thou hath made heaven and earth. Lord, bow down thine ear and hear: open, Lord, thine eyes and see: and hear the words of Sennacherib, which have sent him to reproach the living God. Of a truth, Lord, the kings of Assyria have destroyed the nations and their lands, and have cast their gods into the fire: for they were no gods, but the work of men's hands, wood and stone: therefore they have destroyed them. Now therefore, O Lord our God, save thou us out of his hand, that all the kingdoms of the earth may know that thou art the Lord God, even thou only." (2 Kings xix. 15-20).

And soon the answer came. For Isaiah, the son of Amoz, sent unto Hezekiah saying, "Thus saith the Lord concerning the King of Assyria, He shall not come into this city, nor shoot an arrow there. . . . By the way that he came shall he return. For I will defend this city, to save it, for mine own sake, and for my servant David's sake." (2 Kings xix. 32-34).

Cannot you imagine the deep excitement and suspense over Jerusalem all that week. For surely Isaiah's prophecy was published to the people. Would the Lord save them? How could it be with that countless army of the angry Sennacherib so near as Libnah?

How? We do not know. But one morning all Jerusalem was thrilling with the news. Some great calamity had fallen suddenly on the invading army. Perhaps a pestilence, or a fierce simoon from the desert, or a sudden attack from the army of Terhakah and the Ethiopians. We do not know.

> *The Assyrian came down like the wolf on the fold,*
> *And his cohorts were gleaming in purple and gold;*
> *Like the leaves of the forest when summer is green*
> *That host with their banners at sunset were seen;*
> *Like the leaves of the forest when autumn hath flown*
> *That host on the morrow lay withered and strown.*
> *For the Angel of Death spread his wings on the blast*
> *And breathed in the face of the foe as he passed,*
> *And the eyes of the sleepers waxed deadly and chill*
> *And their hearts but once heaved and for ever grew still.*
> *And there lay the steed with his nostril all wide.*
> *But through it there rolled not the breath of his pride, . . .*
> *And the tents were all silent, the banners alone,*
> *The lances unlifted, the trumpet unblown. . . .*
> *And the might of the Gentile, unsmote by the sword,*
> *Hath melted like snow in the glance of the Lord!*

Yes; the poor stupid conqueror had found out after all that there was One stronger than he. Suddenly and hurriedly he departed. Never again did he lift up spear against Judah nor come into her borders. And perhaps that equally stupid Judah found out something too about the patience and presence of the living God.

(Read 2 Kings xviii. 13, to end of ch. xix.; 2 Chronicles xxxii.)

QUESTIONS FOR LESSON XX

Who was Sennacherib and what did he want in Palestine?

Who was Rab-shakeh?

Tell of his controversy before the walls of Jerusalem.

What request did the Jews make to him?

Show how he dishonoured God.

Did he know what Hezekiah had done to the brazen serpent?

Tell of Hezekiah's prayer and the answer.

What happened to the Assyrians?

KING JOSIAH AND THE FINDING OF THE BOOK OF THE LAW

2 Kings XX. 1-11 and 21 and

parts of XXII., XXIII. and

of 2 Chronicles XXXIV.

§ 1. Manasseh

There is not space to tell in full the rest of the story of Hezekiah. After the deliverance from Sennacherib he was very sick, sick unto death. On his deathbed he prayed earnestly to God to let him live a little longer. You see in his day death would be a very dreary thing. The day had not yet come when "Jesus Christ brought life and immortality to light through the gospel." Hezekiah would only think of a poor lonely ghost going shivering out into the dark unknown. Thank God death for us is very different. Hezekiah's prayer was heard, and Isaiah was sent to tell him that fifteen years were added to his life. Many a man in our day has asked the same thing without success, and we sometimes think that God is hard on us because He does not grant it. Ah! God knows best, and a few more years of this life may be a poor exchange for the loss of these years in the Unseen. It is not always good for us to live longer. It was not for Hezekiah. He was very glad and thankful. He thought it was a great boon; but it was not. For in these fifteen years he married and a son was born to him, who was the greatest curse that the nation ever had. His name was Manasseh, and he became king after his father. He exceeded in every kind of wickedness the worst kings that had gone before him. He even tried to destroy all good out of the land. He put the Ark out of the Holy of Holies, he defiled the altars, he actually blotted out the name of God from all national inscriptions. Then he started a fierce and bloody persecution against the prophets and priests of the Lord, till Jerusalem ran with their blood. Most horrible of all, he put to death the aged Isaiah, the great prophet of Judah and his father's lifelong friend. The Jewish traditions tell that Isaiah had to flee from his fury and hide in a hollow cedar tree, which miraculously closed around him to protect him, and that the executioners followed him and sawed down the tree, cutting the prophet asunder in the midst. The Bible makes no mention of this, but it was a common belief, and I think the writer of the Epistle to the Hebrews had it in mind when he wrote of the heroes of faith who "were stoned, who were sawn asunder," etc. (Hebrews xi. 37).

The Book of Chronicles (xxxiii. 12) says that

Manasseh repented when he was in trouble. But he was a wretched creature not worth discussing further, as was also his son Amon who succeeded him. It is a relief to get clear of them both and turn to the next king, the best and noblest of all the Kings of Judah. Again the question rises, "How such a high type could come of such a low type of father?" And again I try to guess the answer. I think again it must have been his mother who made the difference. The mother always matters most, I think. I should not wonder if that is why the Bible usually takes such trouble to put in the mother's name.

§ 2. Two Famous Boys

Now I want to tell you about this King Josiah and another.

In the year 638 B.C. there were two boys in the kingdom of Judah who were destined to be great men in the future. One was a shy, nervous, lonely lad, the son of a priest, Hilkiah, in Anathoth village; the other sat upon the throne of Judah, though he was only eight years old. The lonely boy became Jeremiah the prophet; the boy on the throne was King Josiah. When they were men they did great work for God together. I wonder if they were ever together when they were boys. I think it likely, but we cannot make sure. I find that Jeremiah's father was named Hilkiah the priest; and I find eighteen years later that Hilkiah was the name of the high priest in Jerusalem. This high priest Hilkiah was connected with a most important story about the Bible. I wish we could find out if he were Jeremiah's father. But his was not an uncommon name, so we can only guess about the boys.

* * * * * * * *

Thirteen years have passed; the boys are grown to be young men. The young king, in this thirteenth year of his reign, is living a beautiful life, earnest and religious, trying to be good and to help his people to be good. He is now especially engaged in repairing the Temple and getting it right after the injuries and neglect of the past fifty years. He has around him a band of helpers, his secretary Shaphan, the high priest Hilkiah, the prophetess Huldah, and probably many others who have escaped the persecutions of the two previous reigns, and are now banded together in the cause of reform.

In this same thirteenth year of Josiah a great crisis has come in the life of the other boy, Jeremiah of Anathoth. He seems up to this to have gone on living his quiet lonely life, thinking about the past, dreaming about the future, longing after God; then when he reached full age he was ordained to be a priest. Now suddenly comes to him his "call" from God to be a prophet. I think this means a voice of God in his heart, a deep strong conviction that God wanted him for this. I think it is the sort of call that comes in our own day to a young student in college, a deep desire to be a clergyman, a conviction, or, at least, a strong hope, that this is God's will for him, that God is calling him. In those ancient days I suppose it meant something even more distinct and unmistakable. But I very much want you to feel these Old Testament miracles are going on and much more frequently to-day. And the belief of the Church is shown by the fact that no young clergyman is ordained without being asked if he believes that he has this call from God like Jeremiah's. Read what Jeremiah says, or, perhaps, what his comrade Baruch, of whom we shall hear later on, says (Jeremiah i. 1): "The words of Jeremiah the son of Hilkiah, of the priests in Anathoth, to whom the word of the Lord came in the thirteenth year of King Josiah." Like Isaiah long ago he was afraid of the responsibility. "Ah, Lord, I am too young, I cannot speak for thee." Then God revealed to him a wonderful fact. "Before you were born I had planned this for you to be a prophet to the nations." Is there anything in the whole world would make a man utterly fearless and devoted if that conviction would not?

So Jeremiah began his long life of prophecy, which was to end nearly sixty years later in a lonely exile far away in the land of Egypt. I think, though, that he was always lonely. No doubt he joined King Josiah's reforming party and helped them by his teaching. But he never seems to have had friends or popularity. I wonder if he had been less sad and melancholy would he have helped people better. I think a man might be very determined and earnest and yet not always look at the dark side of things. I don't know. He certainly came in a hard evil time. The princes and society people wanted the gorgeous idolatry and the vile sins of Manasseh's day. The priests and the prophets hated change. The people did not want the trouble of earnest religion. Jeremiah had fearlessly to rebuke them all, and therefore was unpopular with them all. Ah, it was a bad time. Listen to some of his preaching.

"Ah! run ye to and fro through the streets of Jerusalem and seek if ye can find a man, if there be anyone that doeth justly and seeketh truth." (Jeremiah *v.* 1). Listen again:

"A wonderful and horrible thing is committed in the land; the prophets prophesy falsely, and the priests bear rule by these means; and my people love to have it so: and what shall ye in the end thereof?" (Jeremiah *v.* 30, 31). He had to rebuke all, and he was, therefore, lonely and unpopular.

Some men would not have minded being lonely and unpopular. I think Jeremiah was not built that way. He did mind it keenly. "Wherefore came I out of the womb," he asks, "to see labour and sorrow that my day should be consumed with shame?" "Woe is me with whom all the world has strife and contention!" The people that hurt him so much did not know how tender his heart was. "Oh that my head were waters, and mine eyes a fountain of tears, that I might weep day and night for any people." (*ch.* ix. 1).

When you look at the long book of Jeremiah's sermons and prophecies and Lamentations in the Bible, try to remember the sort of man who wrote them, and the sad, lonely life he had to live.

§ 3. An Exciting Discovery

Now comes one of the most important events in the history of Judah. Five years more have elapsed. Five years since young Jeremiah was called of God. Eighteen years since young Josiah was crowned. There is great excitement in Jerusalem. No one can talk of anything but the news from the Temple.

"Have you heard the news?"

"What news?"

"They have found the Book of Moses—the Book of the Law!"

"What? Where?"

"This morning the king sent down Shaphan the scribe to the Temple to settle about the workmen's accounts for cleaning and repairing. After giving up his accounts the high priest said to Shaphan, 'See what I have found amid the rubbish in the Temple chambers.' And he showed him a large parchment roll. 'I have found this Book of the Law in the House of the Lord.' And now the king has summoned a great gathering of all the elders of Judah and Jerusalem to meet him in the Temple for the reading of the Book."

Such was the talk of the town for days. All Jerusalem looked forward with eager anticipation to the day of assembly when the new-found Law Book should be read. At last the day came, and the young king, standing by the pillar in the Temple, read in the ears of the crowd the words of the Book. And a dread and wonder fell upon them as they heard. Do you wonder why they seemed so unfamiliar with it? Why did not they know their Book of Moses better? Or was this Book the Pentateuch as we have it to-day?

I think it was the Book of Deuteronomy that they had found. The king standing by the pillar could not possibly have read the whole Pentateuch.

But in any case the fact of their being unfamiliar with the Book in Josiah's reign would be nothing strange. It was 300 years since King Jehosaphat had sent teachers into the country places to teach the Book of the Law. It was 250 years since the boy King Joash was crowned and the "Book of the Testimony" was laid on his head. Ever since that time we have no mention of it. In the persecutions and troubles of the past fifty years anything might have happened, and Manasseh, who blotted out the very name of Jehovah from all national inscriptions, might very probably have destroyed every copy that he could find, in which case the Temple copy might very probably have been hidden and afterwards lost or forgotten.

Evidently Hilkiah believed that this was the Temple copy that he had found, and when he brought it forth, after being lost for half a century, one cannot wonder that it should read like a new book. In the English Reformation the Bible, which had grown so unfamiliar, seemed very much a new book to the people of that time.

§ 4. The Mission of the Book

At any rate, this Book of the Law or Book of the Covenant gave a new impetus to Josiah's reformation of religion, and the two Judean boys, now in their full manhood, played their parts well. "The king stood by the pillar, and made a covenant before Jehovah to walk before Jehovah and to keep His commandments and His testimonies and His statutes with all his heart and all his soul, to perform the words of this covenant that are written in this book. And all the people stood to the covenant." (2 Kings xxiii. 3).

I think, though the history does not tell us, that Jeremiah helped very much in this reform. I think he was stirred by God to go on a mission through the land enforcing the precepts of this Book of the Law, for he tells us himself (*ch.* xi.) that "The Lord said unto me, Proclaim all these words in the cities of Judah and in the streets of Jerusalem, saying, Hear ye the words of this covenant and do them. For I earnestly protested with your fathers in the day that I brought them up out of the land of Egypt, saying, Obey my voice," etc.

§ 5. King Josiah's Three Sons

But it was too late, alas! for law books or reforms to save this sinful Kingdom of Judah. The people had gone on too long in habits of evil to stop easily now. The current was too strong, the cataracts were too near. Josiah was within twenty years of the fall of the nation. It is sad to think that a noble king such as Josiah probably helped its fall. For thirteen years after the finding of the old Bible he went on bravely with his reform. But I sometimes wonder whether, in all his zeal for reforming the kingdom, he paid attention enough to reforming his own home. I wonder if he did much in the bringing up of his boys.

When he was about forty years old there were three lads. Eliakim was twenty, Jehoahaz was eighteen, and there was a little chap, Zedekiah, just five years old. I wonder who taught the little chap his prayers, or what sort of mother he had. You know it was this horrible Eastern system where a king had several wives and the children were brought up all together in the harem, often amid very undesirable surroundings. These boys had in later life a very sad history of sin and of trouble. When I read the other day about the youngest one, Zedekiah, falling into great sins, and in the end getting his eyes gouged out by the captor, King of Babylon, I could not help wondering was his mother alive then, and did she know of this horror that had fallen on her son, and then I wondered, too, did she or did anyone teach the poor little boy his prayers when he was five years old. I love to think that God takes all these things into account when He judges sinful men.

I may be wrong about Josiah, but I'm generally inclined to suspect some neglect in parents when boys turn out badly.

At last one day, in the midst of his reforms, in the prime of his life, the great Josiah was killed in battle, in a stupid battle where he had no business at all. The two great nations, Egypt and Babylon, as usual, were fighting, and when the strong Egyptian army was passing through Judah to attack the King of Babylon, Josiah foolishly stood up to oppose him. "I do not want to fight with you," said the Egyptian, "Let me pass." "No," said Josiah; "you shall not pass." So they joined battle, and in the battle Josiah was killed, leaving his reforms unfinished, and leaving his three sons orphans. The little one, Zedekiah, was only ten years old then.

Never was such a loss to the Jewish race. Never was a King of Judah more deeply lamented. The Bible tells us that "All Judah and Jerusalem mourned for Josiah. And Jeremiah lamented for Josiah, and the singing men and singing women spake of Josiah in their lamentations unto this day." (2 Chronicles xxxv. 24, 25).

In the next chapter we shall read about those three badly-reared boys of Josiah and how they went down in the crash when the nation fell.

(Read 2 Kings xx. 1-11 and 21, and part of ch. xxii., xxiii.; 2 Chronicles xxxiv.)

QUESTIONS FOR LESSON XXI

What did Hezekiah on his sick bed ask of God?

Was it good for him and his people? Why not?

Why does God sometimes refuse what we pray for?

What do you know of two famous boys, Josiah and Jeremiah?

Tell of the exciting discovery of the Temple Bible.

Tell what you know of Josiah's three sons.

JEREMIAH AND THE LAST KINGS AND THE FALL OF THE NATION

2 Kings XXIII. 31 etc., and parts of XXIV., XXV.

and the portions of Jeremiah referred to.

§ 1. *The Exile King*

We are drawing near to the end, the dark miserable end. Josiah was dead. His three sons waited for the choice of the people as to who should wear the crown. Little either of them thought what a sorrowful future that crown would bring! For some reason the eldest was passed over, and the second son, Jehoahaz, was made king. But scarce was the coronation over, scarce was the mourning for his father ended, when the King of Egypt appeared with his army and captured the young king and put him in fetters (2 Kings xxiii. 33) and carried him away as a captive to Egypt. It is a miserable story. He was not a good king, "He did that which was evil in the sight of the Lord." Yes, but I cannot help remembering that he was only twenty-one and his bringing-up had probably been a very bad one. And I cannot help seeing that, in spite of it all, there was something lovable about him, and that both prophets and people had great hopes of him. The prophet Ezekiel says "he was a young lion, the nations had heard of him, but he was taken in their pit, they brought him with hooks into the land of Egypt." And Jeremiah, who had loved his father and written a lamentation for his death, says of this sorrow now, "Weep not for the dead (Josiah), neither bemoan him, but weep sore for him that goeth away, for he shall return no more nor see his native country." (Jeremiah xxii. 10) Poor boy! only twenty-one, and the first King of Judah who died in exile.

§ 2. Jehoiakim

Then King Pharaoh made king the elder brother, Eliakim, whose name was now changed to Jehoiakim. A right bad fellow he was. I do not wonder that the people had passed him over for Jehoahaz. He remained as a vassal to Egypt, he spent his time in luxury and indulgence, he forced people to build his palace without payment, he degraded his kingdom by idolatry and impurity and tyranny and injustice.

Jeremiah, who gently passes over the sins of the young exile brother, is very stern with him. Listen to his terrible sermon:—

"Weep," he says, "for the young exile king who shall see his native land no more, but—

"Woe unto him that buildeth his house by unrighteousness, and his chambers by injustice, that useth his neighbour's service without wages, and giveth him not his hire. . . Shall thou reign, because thou viest with Ahab? Did not thy father do judgment and justice? then it was well with him. He judged the cause of the poor and needy, then it was well. Was not this to know one? saith the Lord. But thine eyes and heart are but for covetousness, and for shedding innocent blood, and for violence." (Jeremiah xxii. 10-13).

You may guess that Jehoiakim did not like such sermons. Again and again Jeremiah uttered these public rebukes. In fact, a great part of his book seems to be sermons against this evil time and this evil king and people. But it was dangerous work. Another prophet of less influence, named Urijah, had tried it, and the angry king chased him till he fled to Egypt. Then he sent one of his nobles, his own father-in-law, to capture him in Egypt, and they brought him back and murdered him. We should never have heard of this but for that same generous defender of Jeremiah that I told you of before, telling it in his speech afterwards (Jeremiah xxvi. 20).

But Jeremiah would not hold his tongue for that. There were two chief parties in the state at the time, (1) Jeremiah and his religious friends, who had been with him in Josiah's reforms; and (2) opposed to them the party of wicked nobles and princes with some of the hostile priests. The king naturally sided with these against Jeremiah. But I think public opinion was with Jeremiah, even though the people did not like him personally. It is a very wonderful sign of God's ruling in the conscience of men that even a wicked nation who prefer wrong-doing cannot help feeling respect for the man who insists upon the right.

§ 3. Jeremiah's Warning

However, this could not go on for ever without getting Jeremiah into trouble. The great crisis of the fate of the nation was drawing near. If nothing else would save them and make them good, the strong stern love of God would let the captivity come on them, to try if sorrow would change them. So Jeremiah felt the pressure in his heart of God's command. He tells us that:—

"In the beginning of the reign of Jehoiakim the son of Josiah, King of Judah, came this word from the Lord, saying, Thus saith the Lord: Stand in the court of the Lord's house, and speak unto all the cities of Judah, which come to worship in the Lord's house, all the words that I command thee to speak unto them; keep not back a word. It may be they will hearken, and turn every man from his evil way, that I may repent me of the evil, which I purpose to do unto them, because of the evil of their doings. And thou shalt say unto them, Thus saith the Lord: If ye will not hearken to me, to walk in my laws which I have set before you then will I make this house like Shiloh, and will make this city a curse to all the nations of the earth. And the priests and the prophets, and all the people, heard Jeremiah speaking these words in the house of the Lord, And it came to pass when Jeremiah had made an end of speaking all that the Lord had commanded him to speak unto all the people, that the priests and the prophets and all the people laid hold of him, saying, Thou shalt surely die. Why hast thou prophesied in the name of the Lord, saying, This house shall be like Shiloh, and this city shall be desolate without inhabitant? And all the people were gathered unto Jeremiah in the house of the Lord. . . . And they said, This man is worthy

of death; for he hath prophesied against this city, as ye have heard with your ears. Then spoke Jeremiah. . . . saying, The Lord sent me to prophesy against this house and against this city all the words that ye have heard. Therefore, now amend your ways and your doings, and obey the voice of the Lord your God, and the Lord will repent him of the evil that he hath pronounced against you. But as for me, behold, I am in your hand: do with me as is good and right in your eyes. Only know ye for certain, that if ye put me to death, ye shall bring innocent blood upon yourselves, and upon this city, and upon the inhabitant thereof; for of a truth the Lord hath sent me unto you to speak all these words in your ears. Then said the princes and all the people unto the priests and to the prophets; This man is not worthy of death: for he hath spoken to us in the name of the Lord our God."

Then rose up the elders, who made that generous defence which I have twice referred to already, when they quoted the cases of Urijah and of Micah. The result was that Jeremiah escaped with his life.

§ 4. The Potter's Wheel

But it was only for a while. The great empire of Babylon had taken the place of Assyria and was growing greater and greater, and Judah was growing daily more afraid that Egypt would be conquered and that Babylon would be the power to be reckoned with in the future.

With this dread upon them you may guess how unpopular would be Jeremiah's threatening, that unless they very quickly repented Babylon would certainly sweep them away. They were intensely irritable and touchy on this subject, but all the same they would not repent and turn to the Lord. They grew still more irritable and touchy after the great battle of Carchemish, in which Egypt was totally defeated by Babylon, and Jehoiakim had to submit to be a vassal of the King of Babylon.

Then Jeremiah touched the sore spot more sharply. Those Jewish prophets had very impressive ways of teaching. He went down and, I suppose, took some of the leaders of the people with him, to see a potter in the valley working at his wheel. Silently they stood and watched. And when the vessel was marred in his hand the potter made it into another vessel. This, we are told, was to teach that if a nation doomed by God for its evil should return from its evil that God would forgive and make of it something else, something inferior, but still the best that could be made of it. But you notice that this was while the clay was soft. I suppose Jeremiah waited to see if repentance would come. But it did not.

Then came the second lesson before the elders of the people and of the priests. The prophet preached to them a very stern sermon, threatening destruction to the unrepentant nation. While he preached he held in his hand another potter's vessel, finished and baked hard, to show that it was gone too far for changing or improving, and at the close he dashed it into pieces on the ground. "Thus will I do to this place, saith the Lord, and to the inhabitants thereof." And as if that were not enough Jeremiah marched straight from the valley into the Temple court and repeated it all before the priests and people.

Fiercely they rose against him. Pashur, the priest-in-charge, smote him and put him in the stocks for discouraging the people. But it was of no use, for Jeremiah spoke all the more vehemently. Thus saith the Lord: "I will give all Judah into the hand of the King of Babylon, and he shall carry them away captive to Babylon, and shall slay them with the sword. And all you who have prophesied false comfort to my people shall go into captivity and die in Babylon and be buried there." Not a very pleasant speech for the angry listeners.

Poor Jeremiah was put back into imprisonment and fell into very deep depression like John the Baptist in prison after his daring speech to Herod. You can read all this in Jeremiah xviii., xix., xx.

§ 5. *The Scene in the Winter House*

I don't know how soon after this it was that Jeremiah tried another plan. He had a close friend and comrade, Baruch the scribe, who went to prison with him. They both heard in the prison rumours of the political situation outside, but Jeremiah could not get out. So he told Baruch to get parchment and pen and write down the chief of his prophecies against the nation "from the days of Josiah unto this day." So Baruch wrote. And this is the only place in which we can actually see, as it were, the Bible being made. For what Baruch wrote that day in the prison you can read in your Bible to-day. Probably it was Baruch who collected all the sermons of Jeremiah afterwards.

But what did he write for? To try an experiment. "I

cannot get out," said Jeremiah, "so you are to take this book and read it in the ears of all the people on the fast day. It may be they will yet return every one from his evil way, for great is the anger of the Lord towards them."

It was a dangerous thing to do. Baruch had to wait for nearly a year for his opportunity, then he started off "on the fast day." He began by reading it in the scribes' chamber. Then some of the more friendly princes heard of it and sent for Baruch to read it for them.

They were terrified as they heard—terrified at the threatened doom of Jerusalem, terrified, too, I think, at the anger of the king when he should hear of it. They felt that he ought to know. "We will surely tell the king," they said; "but, oh, hide yourselves, you and Jeremiah; let no man know where you are." I don't know how they were to hide if they were prisoners. I suppose they must have got free during the year.

Next comes a very striking scene in the king's chamber in the winter house on a cold December day, with a fire in the brazier burning before him. Into this room the princes came to read Jeremiah's words to the king. It was risky work reading such things to that gloomy, passionate king. But they did it. Jehudi, one of the nobles, read it, while the others anxiously watched the face of the king. More and more angry grew his countenance as he listened, till all four leaves were read. Then he could stand it no longer. They tried to hold him back, but it was useless. Fiercely he snatched the sacred roll of the word of the Lord and ran his penknife through it, till he had cut it into ribands, then he flung the pieces into the fire. He would let them see whether Jeremiah, or, indeed, Jeremiah's God, would frighten him! How dare anyone tell him that the King of Babylon should destroy the place!

Then he sent three princes off post haste to arrest Baruch and Jeremiah for this treason. But we are told the Lord hid them. I wonder should we have lost this Book of Jeremiah out of the Bible if those three princes had caught them that day? At any rate, they did not catch them, and we read that "Jeremiah took another roll and gave it to Baruch the scribe, who wrote therein from the mouth of Jeremiah all the words of the book which Jehoiakim, King of Judah, had burned in the fire, and he added besides to them many like words."

Jehoiakim soon found that his fate was near. He rebelled against Nebuchadnezzar, King of Babylon, and was seized and carried off captive, and Jehoiachin, his son, reigned in his stead. He was little better than his father. Jeremiah did not think much of him. He declared that he was "a despised broken idol, a vessel wherein there was no pleasure." Nebuchadnezzar, for some reason, was angry with him and carried him also off to Babylon with some other captives, and with the plunder of the Temple of the Lord.

§ 6. The Last of the Kings

Then came "the last of the kings," Zedekiah, whom we remember as a little five-year-old boy in the palace of his father Josiah. He was probably a badly brought up boy. At any rate, he turned out an unsatisfactory king. "He did evil in the sight of the Lord." Yes, and he did foolishness too. In spite of Jeremiah's advice, he sided with a stupid political party who planned to rebel against powerful Babylon.

Now we have a curious picture in the Book of Jeremiah. You remember his teaching by means of potters' vessels. Now watch again. The sad-faced prophet, with a wooden yoke on his neck, marching through the streets of Jerusalem, pleading with king and priests and people that they should keep on their necks the yoke of tribute to Nebuchadnezzar lest worse befall them. Some call him a lunatic, some call him a traitor to his country. To him comes another prophet, Hananiah, who seizes and smashes the yoke upon his neck, crying: "Thus saith the Lord, Even so will I break the yoke of the King of Babylon!" The people were delighted with this patriotic prophecy. And poor despised Jeremiah could only sadly reply, "Amen! may the Lord do so! But ah, alas! he will not do so, Hananiah; thou art a false prophet, thou makest the people to believe a lie."

But the popular party prevailed. The king allied himself to Egypt, and soon the Babylonian army was at the gates of Jerusalem. However, the King of Egypt came to the rescue, and the Babylonians had to raise the siege and retire.

Then the popular party was wild with delight. "Ha! we knew it! Jeremiah was wrong! He is a traitor to his country! The Lord has delivered us out of the hands of Babylon!" So poor Jeremiah saw that he had no longer any influence, and that there was no place for him in Jerusalem. So he resolved to retire from public life and end his days on the little farm at Anathoth, where he had wandered long ago a lonely boy. But it was not to be. He was arrested at the North Gate as he went out, and accused of intending to desert to the Babylonian enemy. His triumphant enemies put him in prison. Public feeling was strong against him, and at last, not having the courage to murder him outright, they lowered him down into an old well, where he sunk deep into the mire, and was slowly starving to death. It is suggested that the 69th Psalm was composed by him at the time.

> "Save me, O God, for the waters are come into my soul,
> I sink in the deep mire where there is no standing," etc.

His life was saved only by the kindness of a black man, Ebed-Melech, the Ethiopian eunuch.

§ 7. The Fall of Jerusalem

But nobody has time now to think about Jeremiah. The whole country is in terror. In the tenth month on the tenth day of the month Nebuchadnezzar came back and all his army and encamped against Jerusalem, and built forts against it round about. Jerusalem's day had come at last. It was an awful siege. The huge engines flinging in stones, the battering-rams breaking the walls, the terrible famine in the city, so terrible that even mothers, it is said, ate their children's flesh. Awful, unutterably awful, was the misery of Jerusalem.

At last, on a hot summer midnight, the besiegers stole in through the breaches, and at the dawn of the next morning King Zedekiah was flying for his life with wives and children. But a Chaldean troop chased him and brought him back to the King of Babylon.

A terrible judgment was pronounced for his rebellion. First, his children were slaughtered before his eyes, and then when he had seen the worst that it was possible to see, his eyes were gouged out by the Chaldean executioner.

Within a month the forts were dismantled, the Temple was burned down, the people were carried away into exile, and the city of Jerusalem lay a blackened, desolate ruin. The end had come at last—the only end that was possible. The strong, stern, tender love of God had brought this punishment upon the nation's sin "for their good always." Be sure that all God's punishments are intended for men's good. This awful sorrow brought Israel nearer to God than all its prosperous days. It is a very terrible lesson for all sinners, but a very beautiful lesson, too, that the strong, stern, tender love of the Father will spare His children no pain for ever here or hereafter, and spare Himself no pain for ever here or hereafter to save them from their sins.

So the poor, sad prophet saw the ruin of his nation and the captivity of its people. He stayed behind with the few who were left to look at their lonely, desolate home. The last words we hear of it are his sorrowful lament:—

"How doth the city sit solitary, that was full of people!
How is she become as a widow!
She weepeth sore in the night, her tears are on her cheeks.
Among all her lovers she hath none to comfort her.
Judah is gone into captivity because of affliction.
She dwelleth among the heathen, and findeth no rest.

  *   *   *   *   *   *   *   *

Is it nothing to you, all ye that pass by?
Behold, and see if there be any sorrow like unto my sorrow
Wherewith the Lord hath afflicted me in the day of
  His fierce anger."
      Lamentations of Jeremiah i. 1, 2, 3, 12.

(Read 2 Kings xxiii. 31 etc., and parts of ch. xxiv., xxv.; 2 Chronicles xxxv. 20, xxxvi. The portions of Jeremiah's writings referred to above.)

QUESTIONS FOR LESSON XXII

Was Jeremiah popular? Why not?

Explain his curious parable of the potter's wheel.

Tell how some of his prophecies in the Bible happened to be written.

What did the wicked king do with these prophecies?

What was the final fate of Jerusalem?

What happened to the last of the Kings?

This is the final fall of the Southern Kingdom. Do you remember what happened to the Northern Kingdom?

LESSON XXIII

THE EXILES IN BABYLON

Portions of Isaiah, Daniel and Psalms referred to.

§ 1. Jeremiah's Letter

Thirty years have elapsed. The whole scene is changed, utterly, entirely. Here are the Jews again—no longer on the battlements of Jerusalem or on the green hills of Palestine, but away, far away in the conqueror's land by the banks of the Great Euphrates. It is a land of blazing sun, of brilliant colour, of red-brown desert, and great rich yellow cornfields stretching away to the distant hills. There is the city of Babylon, the wonder of the world. On the top of its lofty battlements four chariots can drive abreast. The palace of the king is seven miles around, the hanging gardens are high overhead. The mighty temple of Bel, 600 feet high, with its broad lines, orange and crimson and gold and blue, is flashing in the eastern sun. Never before have the poor country Jews seen such power, such wealth, such colour and rich barbaric splendour, such hosts of slaves, such busy wharves, such crowded streets,

239

such brilliant processions, satraps, and captains, and pashas, and judges, and counsellors, and all the rulers of provinces, the gorgeous scenes pictured in the Bible story when Nebuchadnezzar set up his golden image on the plain of Dura (Daniel iii.). The whole was so new, so strange, so full of novelty and excitement, that one could imagine them quite enjoying it. Indeed, for a time, in spite of their exile, I do not think that they were very unhappy. They seem to have settled down in communities together, doing hard work for the conqueror, but not being badly treated, at least not worse than the exiles around them from other lands. Some of their young men got into good posts in the Civil Service of Babylon, and were able to be of use to their brethren. Some of their people probably got into trading and farming and did very well. So for some years life was not so hard. You feel this at once as you read Jeremiah's letter to them. I told you that he had stayed behind with the poor people left in Jerusalem. Now I want you to read the very wise, encouraging letter he wrote to the exiles.

"*Thus saith the Lord of hosts, the God of Israel, unto all the captivity whom I have caused to be carried away captive from Jerusalem to Babylon. Build ye houses; and dwell in them; and plant gardens, and eat the fruit of them, and take wives for your sons and give your daughters to husbands, and multiply there, and be not diminished. And seek the peace of the city whither I have caused you to be carried away captive, and pray unto the Lord for it: for in the peace thereof ye shall have peace. . . For thus saith the Lord, After seventy years I will visit you, and perform my good word toward you, in causing you to return to this place. For I know the thoughts that I think toward you, saith the Lord, thoughts of good, and*

*not of evil, to give you hope in your latter end." (Jeremiah
xxix. 4, etc.)*

§ 2. *"By the Rivers of Babylon"*

But after a while things grew harder to bear. Even
at the best it was a miserable thing to be exiles. The
memory of their own dear land with its ruined city
and blackened temple and desolate homes, and its poor,
blind, captive king, was very sore to them. Soon their
own captivity became more severe. The Jews left behind in Jerusalem rebelled, and the angry Babylonians
carried them off to Babylon, and treated both them and
probably their brethren with much severity.

And as the years passed on and they heard the
prophecies of coming deliverance, and saw signs of
a great king coming to attack Babylon, I think they
showed their delight and their desire to see Babylon
destroyed. And this would, of course, not make their
enemies more gentle.

No history is as good as the actual words of an
eyewitness uttered at the time. There was the greatest of
all God's prophets with them in their captivity, though
strange to say no one even knows his name. His sermons
and prophecies are bound up with the Book of Isaiah.
I will tell you about him afterwards, but just now see
what he says about the condition of the poor exiles.

*"This is a people robbed and spoiled; they are snared in
holes; they are hid in prison houses; they are a prey, and none
delivereth. Israel saith, I gave my back to the smiter, and my*

cheek to them that plucked off the hair. I hid not my face from shame and spitting." (Isaiah xlii. 22).

"Desolation and destruction, and famine and the sword, have befallen thee. How shall I comfort thee? Thy sons have fainted; they lie at the top of all the streets. They that afflict thee have said to thy soul, Bow down, that we may go over, and thou hast laid thy back as the street to them that went over." (Isaiah li. 23).

And here is another eye-witness, fiercer and more indignant, looking back on this terrible time.

"By the rivers of Babylon we sat down and wept; yea, we wept when we remembered Zion. For they that led us captive required of us a song. Sing us one of the songs of Zion. How shall we sing the Lord's song in a strange land? O daughter of Babylon, who art to be destroyed. Happy shall he be that rewardeth thee as thou hast served us. Happy shall he be that taketh thy little ones and dasheth them against the rock." (Psalm cxxxvi.).

How terribly they must have suffered when they could say such fierce, revengeful words as those. Surely God would not judge men severely for such words when they were suffering horribly, and when they had never learned the higher teaching of Christ. I have repeatedly tried to impress on you that the Old Testament ideas must not be expected to be as high as those in the New Testament. This poor servant of God was fiercely angry at the cruel wrongs of the captives. No wonder he should want vengeance on the enemy. We know well our Lord would not approve of this prayer. But we know that our Lord would judge him gently for it, since the full light had not yet come into the world. Our Lord says something like this in St. Matthew vi.: "Ye have heard that it was said to them of old time . . . But I say unto you" something higher and nobler.

§ 3. *The Exile's Heroism*

Now comes a very valuable lesson. How wonderfully God deals with men! Often trouble does more good than happiness. That terrible trouble seems to have done more for Israel than all the years of prosperity. Without it I think they would never have been fitted for God's purpose. Their misery brought them back to God. "The nation, as it were, went into retreat and performed penance for its long errors and sins."

Henceforth idolatry had no power over them. Henceforth the presence of God grew more and more real, and we hear much of private prayer and of devotions to God three times a day. Henceforth, too, they had much nobler ideas of God and right and duty. It is perfectly thrilling to read the instances of this. You know the story of Daniel in the lions' den. Daniel was one of the young men in the Civil Service of the Empire. The king signed a decree that if any one asked a petition of any god for thirty days he should be cast into the den of lions. And we are told "when Daniel knew that the writing was signed he went into his house (where the windows were open toward Jerusalem) and prayed to God three times a day as he did aforetime." (Daniel vi. 10). Was not that a grand, daring act? Then comes the story of Shadrach, Mesach and Abednego. King Nebuchadnezzar had threatened them with the burning fiery furnace if they would not worship his golden image. What did they reply? "Our God whom we serve is able to deliver us, and He will deliver us out of thy hand, O King. But if not, be it known unto thee, O King, that we will not serve thy gods nor worship the golden image which thou hast set up." It was a grand faith to be able to believe that God would deliver them, but surely it was an infinitely grander faith to be able to say, "But if not, if we must be burned in the furnace, still we will not do wrong." Have you ever read "Tom Brown's Schooldays"? If not, get it and read it, and read especially the passage where the boys talk enthusiastically about this scene.

Those stories of Daniel and the three young men were not written till very many years after the Captivity. But I think the stories must have been passed on from the mothers to the children ever since the captivity days. Something probably got added to them in the frequent telling, but surely they are in the main true stories and true pictures of the state of mind of the exiles in Babylon.

Another great gain also came from the exile. The people got frightened lest their nation should be entirely lost as the ten tribes of the north were.

So they grew very, very anxious about their scriptures, collecting psalms and prophecies, and rewriting some of their history. I think the story of Moses was written out more fully then from the old records, and some of his laws and regulations largely added to in order to suit the changed times. The Books of Chronicles were written then from the old records that had been preserved. You will notice all through how the writer keeps telling you that he has gathered his history out of the old books of the nation, the Book of Iddo, the Book of God, the Book of the Chronicles of Solomon, etc. I am sure that God's inspiration was guiding His church in all such work. And so gradually the Jewish Bible was growing.

§ 4. The Great Unknown

What of the prophets in those sorrowful days? Did any remain to comfort the poor exiles? Yes, God never left them forsaken. We read of Ezekiel with one community of exiles by the river of Chebar, and his wonderful sermons are much coloured by his surroundings. Then there is Daniel at the court of the king. Later on we shall see Haggai and Zechariah coming back with the exiles, and you know their books of sermons in the end of the Old Testament.

But far above all, was the Great Unknown—that great prophet who did more for the Jews and more for the whole world than any other prophet of the Lord. Is it not strange that we do not even know his name! We shall probably never know it now. His sermons and prophecies are bound up at the end of those of Isaiah, the son of Amoz, from chap. xl. to the end. There is nothing very wonderful in that to anyone who knows the dangers through which the inspired writings passed. Indeed, the wonder is that any of those sheets of prophecies or psalms or history escaped at all.

Why do we believe that chap. xl. to end was not

part of Isaiah's own sermons? Well, everybody does not believe it. It is like this. Suppose you found a volume of sermons by an English clergyman of the reign of Elizabeth, and that the last six sermons of the book were plainly referring to days when there was no king or queen, when Parliament was supreme and when the nation was in deep sorrow over the results of a civil war. Should you not suspect that six sermons of the time of Cromwell had been bound with the others. Very many careful students of Scripture have felt something like this about the close of Isaiah. It seemed so like a different work by a different man. The new writer seems to be preaching during the Captivity, and trying to comfort the people and promising deliverance. Isaiah, the son of Amoz, was killed before the Captivity, and his book is full of stern warnings of captivity to come. The question is not of very much consequence, but the mention of it may help us to understand this Book of Isaiah better. Of course, you see that it would in no way make us think less of God's inspiration if men should bind two sets of prophecies together. Perhaps the name had been torn off the book of the unknown, or perhaps his name also was Isaiah.

Now I want you to see how beautifully he starts to comfort these poor wretched exiles who wanted to dash the Babylonians' heads against the stones. "Comfort ye, comfort ye, my people, saith your God, Speak ye comfortably to Jerusalem, and cry unto her, that her warfare is accomplished, that her iniquity is pardoned, that she hath received of the Lord's hand double for all her sins." (Isaiah xl.).

The years roll on. It is now about 40 years since the Captivity, and the prophet voices amongst the poor exiles are growing fuller and more hopeful. Jeremiah had told them that in seventy years the people would return. Now they see reason to hope that the beginnings of the deliverance would be earlier still.

This great unknown prophet, second Isaiah as he is sometimes called, was evidently a man with a large outlook and a clear intuition.

For years past his eye had been upon a coming leader, Cyrus the Persian. The world was hearing of him. Babylon was growing afraid of him. Like the name of Napoleon Bonaparte in Europe at the beginning of his career, so was the name of Cyrus the Persian to the Medes and Babylonians. The great unknown statesman prophet spoke of him repeatedly. The captive Jews began to watch his progress with wondering hope.

Up to this there had been but the vague hope and the prayer, "O that salvation were come out of Zion. When God bringeth back the captivity of His people then shall Jacob rejoice and Israel shall be right glad."

But now the conviction was growing more and more clear to their great statesman prophet, till at last he burst forth into definite prediction:—

"Thus saith the Lord to his anointed, to Cyrus, whose right hand I have holden, to subdue nations before him and loose the loins of kings, I will go before thee to break in pieces the doors of brass and cut in sunder the gates of iron. For Jacob, my servant's sake, and Israel, my chosen, I have called thee,

though thou hast not known me. I am the Lord, and there is none else; beside me there is no God." (Isaiah xlv.)

These are just little specimens of the comfort and hope and promise that the great unknown prophet brought to the poor captives just because God had taught him the deep lesson which the elder Isaiah had learned in the days of Sennacherib, that kings and armies and powers of earth were but as little instruments in the hands of God to punish or to reward or to help men.

§ 5. *The Last Night of Babylon*

Five years more have elapsed. The crisis has come. It is the last night of Babylon! The power of Cyrus had been steadily drawing nearer. For a long time he had been trying to capture the city, but the mighty walls and the hundred brazen gates and the defence of the great river made it seem utterly hopeless. How he ever got in nobody can tell. If ever there was a city that seemed absolutely safe, that city was Babylon.

We have some histories not easy to reconcile with each other. We have a Greek history telling that Cyrus turned aside the course of the river, and then in the darkness of night his army crept in by the dry river bed and surprised the city. We have not long since found a clay cylinder in Babylonia, the "Cylinder of Cyrus," giving another account. And we have that wonderful vivid story in the Book of Daniel written many years after the event, but doubtless from earlier accounts handed down amongst the Jews.

It tells us that "Belshazzar the King made a great feast to a thousand of his lords," and all the ladies of his harem and all the gay society of Babylon was present. The siege had gone on so long that they had grown quite secure within the walls of their mighty fortress. And to their revelry they brought the golden vessels which Nebuchadnezzar had taken long ago out of the Temple of Jerusalem, and they drank wine out of the vessels and praised the gods of gold and silver and brass and iron and wood and stone. It was a gay scene of feasting and wild revelry, and I daresay drunkenness and sin.

Suddenly there is a pause, a frightened cry, a deep horror over the whole assembly. The king, with white staring face, is pointing to a mysterious inscription on the wall. Nobody could read it. Everyone was frightened at it. Then the queen-mother rose in her place and told of the Hebrew seer who was of the children of the captivity, who was wiser than all the Chaldean soothsayers and magicians. So they brought in Daniel, perhaps from his lonely watch tower, where he studied the stars and learned deep wisdom.

"What does this awful thing, MENE: TEKEL: UPHARSIN, mean?" they asked him. And he taught them the same old lesson that the two Isaiahs had taught, the lesson which his nation had been learning for centuries— that all kings and great people were but instruments in the hands of God, that God was behind all history. "O thou king, the most high gave to Nebuchadnezzar thy father the kingdom and greatness and glory and majesty. But his head was lifted up, and God's judgment fell on him. And thou his son, O Belshazzar, hast not humbled thyself, but hast lifted up thyself against the Lord of heaven, and the God in whose hand thy breath is, and whose are all thy ways, hast thou not glorified. This is the reading of the strange inscription: Thou art weighed in the balance and art found wanting. Thy kingdom is given to the Medes and Persians." Then the exciting story stops abruptly with these words: "In that night was Belshazzar, King of the Chaldeans, slain." (Daniel v.)

So in a night the city of tyrants fell, and in the morning Cyrus was master of Babylon.

(Read the portions of Isaiah, Daniel and Psalms referred to.)

QUESTIONS FOR LESSON XXIII

Where were the captive Jews carried to?

What do you know of Jeremiah's letter to them?

Find out in the Psalms one of their angry songs of trouble.

Tell briefly their brave story of the fiery furnace.

Tell of "The last night of Babylon."

THE RETURN OF THE EXILES

Parts of Ezra and Nehemiah referred to.

(See end of Lesson.)

§ 1. Cyrus

"Babylon is fallen! Babylon is fallen!" In the captive quarters in Chaldea, in far distant Jerusalem, among the exiles in Egypt, wherever there was a Jewish village or a Jewish man or woman, over the Eastern world, the message flew along. It was received in triumph and delight. They talked of nothing else for months together. And then they began to ask themselves, "What next?"

Aye, what next? For it seemed as if the captives had but exchanged one master for another. They were still captives. Then gradually one and another of the captive nations began to talk of the kindness of the conqueror and his merciful policy to send them all home again to be his friends and servants in their own lands. Thus the other histories outside the Bible tell of the wise plans of Cyrus.

But the Jewish history sees the hand of the Lord in all these things. I have already repeatedly pointed out to you that difference between the inspired Jewish historians and others. They had the clear intuition, the vision of God. By faith they saw God's hand in all life. God's dealing with your own nation is just as close and as miraculous. It scarcely differs at all from His dealing with the Jews. But the Jewish historian saw that, and our historians very often do not. They see how political causes and national jealousies and the good or evil impulses of individuals affect history. But frequently they do not see that God stands behind all history, overruling men's acts in accordance with His purposes. The historian or newspaper writer of our day would say that Cyrus was moved by kindness of heart, or by this or that political motive. And they might be quite right. But the inspired historian saw something further behind that. Listen:—

"Now in the first year of Cyrus, that the word of the Lord might be accomplished, the Lord stirred up the spirit of Cyrus that he made a proclamation through his Kingdom and put it in writing:—

THUS SAITH CYRUS KING OF PERSIA: ALL THE KINGDOMS OF THE EARTH HATH THE LORD GOD OF HEAVEN GIVEN ME . . . WHOSOEVER THERE IS AMONG YOU OF ALL HIS PEOPLE HIS GOD BE WITH HIM AND LET HIM GO UP TO JERUSALEM WHICH IS IN JUDAH, AND BUILD THE HOUSE OF JEHOVAH THE GOD OF ISRAEL WHICH IS IN JERUSALEM. AND WHOSOEVER IS LEFT IN ANY PLACE WHERE HE SOJOURNETH LET THE MEN OF HIS PLACE HELP HIM WITH SILVER AND GOLD AND GOODS AND BEASTS BESIDE THE FREE-WILL OFFERING FOR THE HOUSE OF GOD WHICH IS IN JERUSALEM (Ezra i. 1).

I wonder how Cyrus learned this about God. How did God stir up his spirit? I wonder did Daniel or some of the Jewish officials show him the prophecies with his name, and did this greatly influence him? Or did he merely think it good policy to fall in with the ideas of the different nations? I hope it was the first. I think the Bible leads us to believe that this central man of the world of that day had learned some such high thought as this that God was over him and observing his ways.

§ 2. *The Return*

This edict was issued in the year 568 B.C., the first year of Cyrus, and immediately all over the Jewish settlements went the royal heralds proclaiming freedom to the captives. And immediately the prophets and patriots began to rouse their comrades, "Come back, let us build Jerusalem! let us restore the Temple of the Lord!"

It was a good deal disappointing. They were not at all in such a hurry to go. Some had risen to good positions in trade and in government posts. Many had grown old in Babylon, and did not care to face the risks and privations of the journey. They had probably talked as loudly as any when there was no chance of going. But now it was different.

However, there were many ready to go, strong and young and enthusiastic and full of hope. "Even all whose spirit God had stirred to go up to build the house of the Lord which is in Jerusalem." They were led by Prince Zerubbabel, the last of the royal house of David, and with him Joshua, the High Priest. "And Cyrus the king brought forth the vessels of the house of the Lord which Nebuchadnezzar had brought out of Jerusalem and had put in the house of his gods. And he numbered them to Sheshbazzar, Prince of Judah." (Ezra i. 1). So they set forth.

Now try to put yourself in their place. Can you not imagine the delight of that wonderful day when the procession of 40,000 exiles started from Babylon, the young men, proud and enthusiastic, falling into the ranks, the princes and leaders praying to the Lord, the old men and women who stayed behind in Babylon sobbing as they saw the brave procession move off. "Go ye forth out of Babylon," their great prophet had said, "flee ye from the Chaldeans, with a voice of singing declare ye, tell ye, utter ye to the end of the earth; say ye, The Lord hath redeemed his servant Jacob. And the ransomed of the Lord shall return and come with singing unto Zion, and everlasting joy shall be on their heads; they shall obtain gladness and joy, and sorrow and sighing shall flee away." (Isaiah xlviii. 20; li. 11).

And so they did. Listen to one of the songs of the return:—

> "When the Lord turned again the captivity of Zion
>   We were like unto them that dream.
> Then was our mouth filled with laughter,
>   And our tongue with singing:
> Then said they among the nations,
>   The Lord hath done great things for them.
> The Lord hath done great things for us;
>   Whereof we are glad.

Turn again our captivity, O Lord,
   As the streams in the south.
  They that sow in tears shall reap in joy."
                  Psalm cxxvi.

Thus they felt as they started for home.

§ 3. *"His Mercy Endureth For Ever"*

On they went day after day, feeling surely like their ancestors of old marching through the desert to the Promised Land. At last they saw the plains of Syria. Then the white hills of Hermon broke upon their sight, the first view of the dear old country. Then another and another of the well-known landmarks were pointed out by the older men who remembered them. Then at last came the morning when they mounted the last hill-slope and the broken towers and domes of the Holy City, the city of their dreams, stood out upon the far horizon.

Who can tell what that moment meant to them? We read in the story of the Crusades how these warriors of Europe fell on their knees and actually wept with emotion as Jerusalem first broke upon their view. Ah! it would mean much more to the Jewish exiles. Then at last they entered the Holy City, and poor dead Jerusalem became alive with joy.

I do not doubt that after the first excitement and enthusiasm there must have been disappointment. The poor Jews who had been left behind were a dispirited little crowd. The Temple was a ruin, the city walls were broken down. Of all the old kingdom of Israel only a little strip near Jerusalem remained to them.

But if they were disappointed it did not baulk their great purpose, the restoring the Temple of God. We have in Ezra iii. a vivid picture of the day of laying the foundations, the smoke rising from the altar, the richly-robed priests with the silver trumpets, the cymbals clashing in the hands of the sons of Asaph. And in the midst of the joyous service they sang one to another in praising and giving thanks unto the Lord, "for His mercy endureth for ever." Should not you like to search through the Psalms to find the psalms of that day? Look at the 106th, 107th, 118th. Look especially at the 136th, and hear the priests chanting the verses, and the choir responding:—

> "O give thanks to the Lord, for He is good:
> *For His mercy endureth for ever.*
> O give thanks unto the God of gods:
> *For His mercy endureth for ever.*
>
> *　　*　　*　　*　　*
>
> Who remembered us in our low estate:
> *For His mercy endureth for ever.*
> And hath delivered us from our adversaries:
> *For His mercy endureth for ever.*
> O give thanks unto the God of gods:
> *For His mercy endureth for ever.*"

Thus they sang and shouted of their joy unto the Lord. But I think it is very touching to read that the old men who had seen the glory of the first Temple wept with a loud voice at this poor little beginning, "so that the people could not discern the noise of the shout of joy from the noise of the weeping." I like to think how the heart of God would be touched at the mingled rejoicing and weeping that day.

§ 4. Haggai and Zechariah

But after all the excitement and enthusiasm came chill and disappointment, and some hindrances. That is often so in life, so we must not lose heart at it. The first trouble was from the inhabitants. The inhabitants of the land came, the mixed race of Jews and Assyrians who had married with each other. "Let us help you to build the Temple," they said, "for we too seek your God."

I wish they had let them, though they were stupid and ignorant and half heathen. I think it was very stiff and unkind to turn these poor Samaritans off because they were not pure Jews. I am sure our Lord would not like it. You remember how kind He was to the Samaritans? But the proud, earnest Jews had not our Lord's teaching. "Ye have nothing to do with us," they said. "We ourselves together will build unto the God of Israel."

So the Samaritans got angry and tried to interrupt the work, and sent complaints to Babylon against the Jews. This delayed the work. But worse than this was that many of the richer Jews got careless about it and began to make excuses. "This is not the time for building the Temple. The seventy years that Jeremiah prophesied of are not accomplished." It was only an excuse to keep their money to build beautiful houses for themselves.

Then arose two more prophets. Jeremiah was dead, and Ezekiel. And I suppose the great unknown prophet of the Captivity was dead too. Then came these two. You have seen the little books of Haggai and Zechariah in that bundle of prophetic writings all jumbled together at the end of the Old Testament. Now pick them out and place them just here, and you will see exactly where they fit in. Haggai was, I think, an old man who wept for the first Temple. Zechariah was of the younger generation. They were both in the little crowd that came up from Babylon.

Zechariah seems the greater prophet, and he taught great lessons of righteousness. He was an optimist, who could see beautiful visions of Jerusalem's future. But I like Haggai best. He does not seem very clever or eloquent or deep thinking, but I enjoy the practical way, in which he "goes for" these covetous Jews who were making excuses for not helping the Temple building. Look at his first sermon before leaders and people (Haggai i.): "Thus saith the Lord of hosts, this people are saying it is not the time for the Lord's house to be built. Is it a time for you yourselves to dwell in your ceiled houses while this house lieth waste? . . . Thus saith the Lord, Go up to the mountain and bring wood, and build the house, and I will take pleasure in it," etc. You should read the whole sermon. It was a right good sermon, and had a right good effect. "The people did fear before the Lord. And the Lord stirred up the spirit of Zerubbabel and the spirit of Joshua the high priest and the spirit of all the remnant of the people, and they came and did the work in the house of the Lord.

So at last, after nearly twenty years of delay from hostile Samaritans and careless Jews, the Temple was finished on the third day of the month Adar, the month of March, B.C. 516. And again there was a joyful festival service and a great Passover like the great Passover of Hezekiah long ago, and the singing of the joyful Psalms of Haggai and Zechariah, the four Psalms which close the Psalter.

> *Praise ye the Lord,*
> *Praise God in His sanctuary;*
> *Praise Him in the firmament of His power.*
>
> * * * * *
>
> *Praise Him upon the loud cymbals,*
> *Praise Him on the high-sounding cymbals;*
> *Let everything that hath breath*
> *Praise the Lord.*

§ 5. *Ezra*

Now comes a blank in the history for about seventy years. Remember Ezra had not yet come.

Up to this we have been studying the Book of Ezra to chapter vii. The book was written, I feel sure, by the writer of the Books of Chronicles, for you see the last words of 2 Chronicles are repeated again in the beginning of the Book of Ezra to connect the story. At any rate, at chap. vii. he skips over seventy years to tell of a second "Return from Babylon" under Ezra the Scribe, who brought a letter from the great King

Artaxerxes. And at chap. viii, he lifts bodily into his history Ezra's own story of the events in Ezra's own words, "the genealogy of them which went up with *me*."

We know nothing of those seventy years. Things seem to have settled down from the great excitements and enthusiasms into the ordinary humdrum life of a large country town, buying and selling and marrying Jews with Jews, and also with Samaritans.

Suddenly Ezra comes with a second band from Babylon, and he comes, he says, very beautifully, "because of the good hand of my God come upon me." He comes with a good deal of wealth to help the poor colony, and above all with a full complete copy of the Torah or Law of Moses. They seem to have had only parts of it in Jerusalem. Probably there were less and more complete editions of it. Probably the prophets and priests and holy men amongst the exiles in Babylon had edited it and completed it by adding many ordinances fitted for their own time. I have repeatedly pointed out to you how the Old Testament historians keep telling us that there was a "Bible before the Bible," a set of older books now lost, that they had re-written the history from these older books, and that the now long lost books of "Jasher" and of the "Wars of the Lord" and the "Chronicles of God" and of "Iddo the Seer" and many others were the authorities from which they worked. Probably the Law of Moses was in the same way at various times edited and completed to bring it up to date. Whatever Moses left could not have been otherwise than very incomplete for the needs of the nation afterwards.

Whether it was for this reason, or because the Jews in Jerusalem had become careless about the study of the Scripture, Ezra's Book of the Law seemed to him the most important thing that he had brought to Jerusalem. Yet somehow he does not seem to have succeeded in teaching it much for a long time. I sometimes think that he began badly, and so got up a hostile feeling against him.

He tells us in chap. ix. how utterly horrified he was to learn that many of the princes and priests and people had intermarried with the heathen people of the land. To him it seemed a very awful thing. And it certainly was, if the people of the land were all of the type of the filthy idolators whom we read of in the days of the kings. But I cannot help thinking of those Samaritans who had offered to help at the Temple building seventy years before, and said that they, in their ignorance, were trying to seek God. Perhaps it was some like those they had married. And perhaps Ezra, in his great zeal for God and for the purity of the race, was a little bit narrow and harsh, like the Jews who had repulsed those Samaritans. I do not think he had a wife or children himself. At any rate, he strictly ordered in the name of God an utter separation from these wives and families.

There is a very pitiful scene in chap. x. 12. The whole congregation answered, "As thou hast said so must we do. But the people are many, and it is a time of much rain, and we are not able to stand outside. So let there be an appointed time to go over the whole list of the men who have done this."

Perhaps Ezra was right. I cannot judge. But I know that good and holy men do sometimes harsh things, and I should like to hear what all the cast-off wives and children had to say, before I tried to guess whether he was right or wrong. At any rate, he does not seem to have got on much with his teaching of the Law till another leader came about fourteen years later.

§ 6. Close of Old Testament Story

The new leader, Nehemiah, tells us his own story (Nehemiah i.). He was an important official, a sort of house steward, in the palace at Shushan. One winter day he was visited by some men out of Judah, and they told him of the poor state of the city, with its affliction and reproach, with its broken walls and its enemies all around.

So, he says, I wept and fasted and prayed to God, and on my next appearance before the king he noticed my sadness. "Why is thy countenance sad?" asked the king. I told him. "For what dost thou make request?" he asked. So I prayed to the God of Heaven, *i.e.* (lifted up my heart for a moment), and I told the king. Then follows the story of the king's consent and how he sent him off with a royal guard and gifts and letters to the chief officers to supply materials. Then the story of his arrival in Jerusalem and the building and dedication of the walls.

And then chap. viii., a wonderful scene in which Ezra appears again. It was at the Feast of Tabernacles, and "all the people gathered themselves together as one man to the broad place before the Water Gate, and they spake to Ezra the Scribe, to bring the Book of the Law of Moses, which God had commanded Israel." And then we see Ezra mounting his pulpit of wood, and unrolling the great roll of the Law in the sight of that great crowd, and when he opened it all the people stood up and Ezra blessed the Lord and His servant Moses, and all the people answered, Amen, Amen, with lifting up of their hands; and they bowed their heads and worshipped the Lord." And Nehemiah, the Tirshatha or governor, and Ezra the priest, and the Levites comforted the people . . . and there was great gladness, and they kept the feast seven days, and day by day from the first day unto the last day he read in the book of the law of God.

And thus we leave them, the poor penitent people of God and their two great leaders praying together and studying God's Word. And thus the Old Testament story closes. How better could it close? There is much more to be told of—troubles and wars and persecutions and the grand brave fight under the Maccabees; but the Old Testament does not tell of these things. So the story closes, to open again 400 years later, "when Jesus was born in Bethlehem of Judæa in the days of Herod the King."

(Read parts of Ezra i., ii., iii., iv., v., ix., x., and parts of Nehemiah i., viii.)

QUESTIONS FOR LESSON XXIV

Did the exiles ever come back to their own land?

Who sent them back?

Find out in the Bible their triumphant song of thanksgiving.

What do you know of (1) Haggai, (2) Zechariah, (3) Ezra, (4) Nehemiah?

Tell of Nehemiah's little prayer and how he got leave from the King.

Describe the scene of the great Bible reading before the Water Gate.